So You Want to Be a Teacher?

Mary C. Clement

A SCARECROWEDUCATION BOOK

The Scarecrow Press, Inc.
Lanham, Maryland, and London
2002

A SCARECROWEDUCATION BOOK

Published in the United States of America
by Scarecrow Press, Inc.
A Member of the Rowman & Littlefield Publishing Group
4720 Boston Way, Lanham, Maryland 20706
www.scarecroweducation.com

4 Pleydell Gardens, Folkestone
Kent CT20 2DN, England

British Library Cataloguing in Publication Information Available

Library of Congress Cataloging-in-Publication Data Available

ISBN 0-8108-4219-X

∞™ The paper used in this publication meets the minimum requirements of
American National Standard for Information Sciences—Permanence of
Paper for Printed Library Materials, ANSI/NISO Z39.48-1992.
Manufactured in the United States of America.

This book is lovingly dedicated to Zebulon,
the cat whose unconditional love and adoring attention have
helped me to survive and stay balanced since 1997.

Special thanks to my students at Berry College in northwest Georgia
who have shared their reasons for becoming teachers with me,
while also sharing their joys and concerns about
entering this wonderful profession.

Contents

Introduction

For 13 years you sat in classrooms, as a student, and watched teachers do their work. Because of this you know a lot about what teachers do. You know that teachers take attendance. They turn this attendance in to someone in the office. You know that some teachers are responsible for lunch counts and milk money.

Go back in time to kindergarten, first, second, and third grade and think of all the things those early teachers did for you. Your teachers probably made sure that you had the right books at the right time. (How did they decide which books?) Somebody made sure that you got to lunch on time and had bathroom breaks between the start of school and noon. Did your early teachers teach you reading, writing, mathematics, and science? Did they teach you about the big world? (Let's count this as social studies.) Did they teach you to memorize your address and phone number? And not to talk to strangers? Did your elementary teachers prepare you for the big jump to middle school? Was it called junior high then? (What's the difference, any-way?) Did they teach you to draw and paint and sing and maybe even dance? If your teachers couldn't sing or dance, did they at least play music for you and teach you about that kind of music? Did they tell you about faraway places that you had never heard of before their class? Did your teachers teach you about what to eat and how to play games? Did a teacher introduce you to soccer or baseball or basket-ball or hangman or the rules to volleyball? Did a teacher make you feel good about yourself on a lousy day? Did a teacher ever make you feel lousy?

YOUR LIST OF TEACHERS

How many teachers taught you before that big jump to the middle school or junior high? Then how many taught your classes in middle grades and did they teach you to be ready for high school? How many teachers taught your classes in high school? How many can you remember? Stop now and make that list. Write the grade and/or subject. Many of us were taught by 40 to 60 teachers from kindergarten through high school. It will probably be easier to list the teachers in chronological order. Make your list like this:

Year in school	Teacher's name	More categories will follow
Kindergarten	Terry	

Allow lots of space between the teachers. We will add categories and later we will look at this list for several other reasons.

MIDDLE SCHOOL

Let's talk a minute about these unique middle years between elementary school and high school. For some of us, those years were maybe sixth, seventh, and eighth grade in what was called a middle school. For others, we were in a true junior high that had the divine mission of preparing us for high school. Did you have teams of teachers? Did you move from room to room or did the teachers move or did you stay with one teacher all day? Do you remember being all "hormones on legs" during these years? Which classes did you enjoy then? Did you get involved in sports or band or chorus or art or any kind of club at this time? Did you start studying a foreign language or computers? Did you go to after-school events and see your teachers? Did your teachers know your name and did they help you get through any major traumas—like your boyfriend or girlfriend dumping you, or pimples, or something equally horrifying?

HIGH SCHOOL

Then there was high school. What did you study in high school? *Did* you study in high school? Did you work at a paying job while in high school? Did you date? A lot? Did you participate in sports? Marching band? Chess club? Cheerleaders? Technology club? French club? Did you get married or have a baby in high school? Did any of your friends? Do you still keep in touch with any of your friends from high school? With any of your teachers? What did you learn in high school? Were you prepared for "the real world" when you graduated? Did you feel prepared to be an adult? Do adults need to know algebra? Calculus? Spanish? World civilization? American history? What was your best class in high school? Was the teacher of this class your favorite teacher? Was he or she effective?

YOUR TEACHERS

By watching teachers do their work for 13 years you should be an expert at what teachers do, shouldn't you? They teach. Yes, right, and they grade papers and give grades and sometimes they break up fights in the hallway. They get to cut in line in the cafeteria to get food and *they* get to bring coffee into the classroom in some schools. They have the summers off (wow) and they work from about 8 A.M. to about 3:30 P.M. Except the coaches. Apparently the coaches work from 8 to 3:30 then they go to practices and turn kids into athletes. But that is so much fun that they probably don't mind. It would be fun to coach a team, wouldn't it?

Were your teachers men or women? In elementary school, were there any men who were teaching? How about middle and high school? Go back to your list of teachers now and add up how many men and how many women worked as your teachers. While you are looking at the list, count up the numbers of white teachers, African American teachers, Asian teachers, Hispanic, and other racial/ethnic cultures represented by your group of teachers.

Let's do one last thing with that list of teachers at this point. Beside each teacher's name, mark if you would rehire that teacher based upon your experience in his/her class at the time when you were in the class. For example, your list may look like this now:

Year in school	Teacher's name	M/F	Ethnicity	Rehire?
Kindergarten	Tallen	F	W	Yes
First	Nelson	F	W	Yes
Second	Luz	F	Hispanic	Yes

Now, and most important, would you want to do the job that someone on this list did? At this point, do you want to be a third-grade
teacher like your third-grade teacher appeared to be? Are you interested
in being a seventh-grade science teacher like your seventh-grade science teacher was? Do you want to teach and coach a high school sport?
Are any of your parents, relatives, neighbors, or close friends on your
list? Do you happen to know a lot about any of the people on your list?
Do you know how much money they made when they were your
teacher? Are they still teaching? Did anyone get fired and then sue the
school because of being fired? Do you know where your teachers went
to college and studied to become teachers? Did any of your teachers
love teaching? How do you know? Did any of them win awards for
their teaching? Did any of them have after-school or summer jobs? Did
these teachers have children of their own? Did their children go to the
school when you did? Did any of your teachers become principals? Superintendents? College professors? Where are they now?

YOUR PERSONAL TEACHING BACKGROUND

One of my college professors said that there were no "throw-away" experiences in life. He meant that each of us is changed, touched, affected, or
maybe even scarred by the experiences that we have had. The teaching
profession is a unique one because you have seen teachers in their work
environment for 13 years. Is there any other profession or job where you
have seen the worker this "up close and personal"? In recent years we
have seen the growth of "take your daughters to work" days and of mentoring programs to show young people what workers actually do, but
these days are isolated and not like watching the workers for 13 years.

By watching teachers in their world for so many years, you, and the rest
of the general public, have definite opinions about what teachers do. By
being a member of "the general public," you also have heard and read
many things about teachers—their salaries, their complaints, their concerns, and possibly the violence in their classrooms. You may have heard
that teaching is currently a "hot" job with lots of openings and that there
is a teacher shortage. Whether you are an 18-year-old freshman in college
or a 50-year-old considering a job change, you have quite a personal history with teachers. You already have opinions, experiences, and background that will shape your decision to be a teacher and that will shape
your work as a teacher, if you decide to become one.

It is the purpose of this book to help you make the decision whether or not to become a teacher. Choosing to become a teacher is indeed a big decision. However, the more knowledge you have about what teachers do and the context of what today's schools are like, the easier it will be for you to make that decision. There will be explanations of why people choose to become teachers, how to become a teacher, and how to be an effective teacher. The lifestyle of the teacher will be discussed, as well as the life cycle of people who choose this profession. Burnout will be mentioned, as well as the rewards of teaching. As you read about today's students, you can see the growing diversity in the classroom. Many additional resources will be presented, so that you can read widely about your chosen field. This book may answer some of your questions. It will definitely ask you more questions than you ever considered!

ABOUT YOUR LIST OF TEACHERS

You may want to refer back to your list of teachers several times while reading this book. The list made you think about your personal experiences. There were probably more women than men on your list because two-thirds to three-fourths of the pre-school through 12th grade (p–12) teaching force are females. There were probably few African American, Hispanic, or Asian Americans on your list, because white females are the vast majority of teachers. However, today's students are indeed diverse and need effective teachers and role models from all racial and ethnic backgrounds. A goal of school districts continues to be that of creating a teaching faculty that truly represents the diversity of society's population. If you want to be a teacher for any reason—to be a role model, to help children the way that your teachers helped you, or to be a better teacher than some of your teachers—continue to read this book. Through reading, talking with friends, family, and practicing teachers, and by reflecting on your experience and beliefs, you can make an informed answer to the question, "Do I want to be a teacher?"

QUESTIONS/REFLECTIONS

1. From your list of teachers, identify your favorite teacher. Why was he/she your favorite? What did he/she do differently than the other teachers?

2. Was your favorite teacher an effective teacher? What did he/she do that demonstrated effectiveness in the classroom? Did other students like this teacher? Did he/she win awards or seem well liked by the other faculty and administration?

3. Write a letter in support of rehiring your favorite teacher. Pretend your audience is the principal, superintendent, and board of education.

4. Write a letter of thanks to your favorite teacher, asking his/her advice and counsel about your decision to be a teacher.

FAQS FROM STUDENTS CONSIDERING CAREERS IN TEACHING

For several years I have been teaching a course for freshmen in college who are considering teaching as a career. While many of my students are 18-year-olds, the range of ages goes up to age 45. Many of my freshmen are already parents, have already tried other jobs, and have now decided on going to college. At the start of each new course, I ask the students what their personal questions are about teaching. In essence, "What do they want answered by the end of the course?" In addition, I ask, "What do you want answered before you make the plunge and commit to the teacher education program?" Here are the most frequently asked questions by my students.

1. What is the most challenging thing about a teacher's job?

2. Is it true that discipline has become harder to enforce?

3. How difficult will classroom management be?

4. What do you do when you become frustrated with your own students (and their problems)?

5. Are parent/teacher relationships easy/successful?

6. How do you keep students interested in the material?

7. What are the biggest challenges of teaching elementary school?

8. How do I decide which grade to teach?

9. How do I teach a student who doesn't speak English?

10. What are the differences in teaching middle grades and high school?

11. Should I begin teaching after college or get my master's degree first?

12. As a high school teacher, what is the best way to earn the respect of the students?

13. How can I prevent cheating?

14. Which states pay teachers the most?

15. Will I earn more money if I teach high school?

16. How can I teach outside the United States?

17. What do teachers dislike about their jobs?

18. What is expected of me my first year? Do I have to do everything a veteran teacher does, or will I have an easier schedule that first year?

19. How will I know what to organize and teach each semester?

20. If I get certified to teach in this state, can I teach in other states?

21. How many hours a day does a teacher work?

22. How do I keep up with everything if teaching is as hard as some people say it is?

23. How do I get my first job?

24. How do I decide which field to teach?

25. Why do some teachers quit? What do they do next?

Did any of these questions come to your mind? How many of these questions can you answer? There are multiple answers to most of these questions. Keep reading for more insights into these questions. Write three questions that you would add to this list.

CHAPTER 1

Why People Choose Teaching

The number one reason given by elementary teachers for choosing their profession is a love of children (Wiseman, Cooner, & Knight, 1999). This makes a lot of sense. Many elementary teachers are women who grew up "playing school" and babysitting for young children. Historically, teaching school was one of the "appropriate" professions for women to choose, especially for the women who didn't choose to be nurses.

Teaching is considered a "family-friendly" profession. Teachers tend to have the same hours in school as their children. Sometimes children will have to wait in a parent's classroom before or after school, but this is still a compatible schedule, compared to a 70-hour workweek in some offices, where children cannot be seen or heard. Teaching is considered a good choice for a parent because of holiday and summer breaks. Unlike many working parents, teachers do not have to find daycare supervision for their children during these vacations.

The ease of exit and reentry into the teaching profession also makes it more family friendly than some. Most teachers have complete benefit packages that include multiple weeks of maternity and paternity leave. Tenured teachers often have the option of taking one semester or one year of unpaid leave of absence to stay home with a newborn. While each school district is different, many teachers can return to their original classroom or building in the district after their absence. Some teachers choose to quit their jobs to begin families, knowing that when they return in a few years, positions will probably be available.

SECONDARY TEACHERS

Why do secondary teachers choose teaching? A survey of teachers completed by the National Education Association (Ryan & Cooper, 1998, p. 10) found that the three top reasons selected by all teachers for deciding to teach were "desire to work with young people," "value or significance of education to society," and "interest in subject-matter field." Secondary teachers often report that their love of a subject and their desire to share that subject motivates their decision to teach at the high school level. I consider myself typical in this respect. I decided to major in Spanish in college because I felt that I had studied English, math, social studies, and science long enough, from first grade through my senior year in high school. I had only studied Spanish since ninth grade and knew I wanted more, so that's how I picked my major. I added teacher certification as a backup plan.

TEACHING AS A BACKUP PLAN FOR FLEXIBILITY

There are many stereotypes about who becomes a teacher. You may have heard the old saying, "Those who can, do, and those who can't, teach." Those of us in education changed that old adage long ago. We say, "Those who can, teach. Those who can't, go into some other less significant line of work." Perhaps the second-oldest line about teaching is that it is a safe backup plan to add to your college diploma. When I told my high school guidance counselor that I wanted to be a foreign language major, he seemed concerned. He thought for a moment, then said, "Well, I'm going to write Spanish education as your intended major, since I'm not sure what you can do to earn a living with that major here in our little town if you don't teach." While this attitude might seem callous or old fashioned, or maybe even sexist, I now say, "Bless you, Mr. Thaxton."

FLEXIBILITY IN MOVING

My backup plan was getting a teaching certificate, and that plan led me to a wonderful career. My "backup" plan is also indicative of why teaching can be such a good career choice for a man or woman. Teachers are needed in urban areas, medium-sized cities, and small towns. If one spouse is a teacher, he/she is going to be able to relocate with more flexibility than some careers. For example, my husband is a television engineer, and at the level of engineering that he does, his best job prospects are in New York, California, or Atlanta. When we moved from a medium-sized midwestern town (small TV station) to metro-Atlanta, I knew I could find a teaching position.

A friend of mine is in an upper administrative position at a college. In order to increase her job prospects, she will probably need to move every four to six years until she is a college president. Her husband, an elementary teacher, has excellent job prospects wherever they relocate.

"IT'S A NICE SECOND INCOME"

While we're talking about myths and old sayings surrounding the teaching profession, you have probably heard the classic line, "It's a nice second income." Well, teacher salaries continue to rise, as do the benefit and retirement packages offered to teachers. Many state-funded retirement packages offer the opportunity to retire at age 55—a full 10 to 12 years before other jobs. Life insurance, health, dental, and vision benefits are generally offered to teachers, making their overall benefit packages increasingly more attractive. In many families, the spouse who is the teacher secures the health benefits for the entire family because the teacher's package is simply the best available.

Find out about current salaries and benefit packages in your area. Anything written here would be outdated before this book was actually published, so go to the Internet and look at salaries for your state. Teacher salaries are public knowledge and are probably posted in your local newspapers, too.

In my own work with graduate students who already had a bachelor's degree and who were returning to college for teacher certification, I have found that their primary reasons for choosing teaching are salary and benefits. Many of these students have told me that their current job paid much less than teaching and required weekends and late hours that took them away from their families. Many people, both male and female, choose to teach after having worked in other careers, and they tend to say their decisions were based on balancing their incomes with family needs and childcare concerns.

In his talks, noted educator Harry K. Wong reminds us that teachers are not poor and downtrodden. He writes that "If you are a new teacher: You have a magnificent future awaiting you, with teaching positions and educational opportunities galore" (Wong & Wong, 1998, p. iv). The positives of teaching are definitely to be found, in salary, benefits, and personal validation.

Do high school teachers make more money than their counterparts in elementary school? "No" is the answer to that question. School districts have teacher salary schedules and the beginning salaries are based upon degrees earned and years of experience. For example, a new second-grade teacher with a bachelor's degree and no experience will have the same salary as a new high school math teacher with a bachelor's degree and no experience. A fourth-grade teacher with 20 years of experience and a master's degree will indeed make more money than a high school teacher with only 10 years of experience and no master's degree. A few school districts have experimented with incentives to get teachers in fields considered "high demand," such as special education and math and science. However, most schools have faculties that are members of one of the two national teachers' organizations, and these organizations bargain contracts for teacher salaries. Some states have minimum salaries for all teachers and a statewide teacher pay scale. In other states, each district sets its own salaries in negotiation with the teachers' union/organization. The two major teachers' organizations are the National Education Association (NEA) and the American Federation of Teachers (AFT). As you read about salaries in your state, you may find that small rural districts pay much less than large suburban districts. Look at the cost of living in the area that you want to work as well as other factors before making your decision.

A WORD ABOUT MIDDLE SCHOOL TEACHING

So far we have talked about becoming an elementary teacher or a high school teacher, but there is another level of teaching that sometimes gets overlooked—middle grades teaching. Called junior highs from about the 1880s, these schools were historically designed for seventh- and eight-graders as pre-high schools (Callahan, Clark, & Kellough, 1998). Now middle grades are defined by each state, and districts choose to call their schools middle schools or junior highs based on the philosophy of the district. A junior high is generally still a school with a philosophy of preparing students for high school. Teachers in junior highs were probably trained as secondary teachers and may consider themselves subject matter specialists. A middle school teacher may have majored in elementary education or middle grades education. The National Middle School Association offers official positions on middle school philosophy in *This We Believe* and its journals (Callahan, Clark, & Kellough, 1998, p. 13). A middle school may include sixth, seventh, and eighth grades, or only seventh and eighth grades, or another combination from fourth to ninth grades. You will see a wide variety in middle schools and junior highs around the country. Middle school is a much more modern term than junior high, and even saying junior high may date you terribly in some regions. If you are interested in teaching grades four through nine, please read more about middle school certification in the next chapter.

IS THERE REALLY A TEACHER SHORTAGE?

The cover of the October 2, 2000, issue of *Newsweek* read, "Who will teach our kids?" and the story that followed was titled, "Teachers Wanted." The authors of the article made the statement, "With a million veterans ready to retire, school districts are sounding the alarms and calling in emergency recruits to lead our classrooms" (Kantrowitz & Wingert, 2000, p. 37). Harry Wong reminds us that approximately 200,000 new teachers enter the profession each year (1998, p. iv). Southworth (2000, p. 25) reported that "In 1999 the National Education Association stated that two million teachers will need to be hired in the next ten years to fill both current and newly created positions. Recruiting New Teachers, a nonprofit organization in Belmont, Massachusetts, concurs with these projections."

The answer to the question, "Is there a teacher shortage?" may definitely depend on where you live and the field of teaching about which you are talking. In addition to current newspapers and magazines, the *Job Search Handbook for Educators* is a good source of data to answer this question. Published annually by the American Association for Employment in Education in Columbus, Ohio, the handbook contains the association's annual research report, "Teacher Supply and Demand by Field and Region." For example, the 2000 edition of the handbook listed considerable teaching shortages in the areas of special education, bilingual education, and physics, while listing some shortages in the areas of math, speech pathology, other sciences, Spanish, English as a second language, library/media, home economics, gifted education, school psychology, agriculture, and reading. The report listed surpluses in the fields of physical education, health education, and social studies, with all other fields appearing balanced in terms of supply and demand of teachers (AAEE, 2000, p. 13).

Why are there more openings for teachers than ever before in some areas of the country? Early retirement options for state employees account for some of the openings. There are simply more students in schools than ever before, and in some areas, such as the sunbelt states of the southeast and California, the numbers increase dramatically every year. Some states (California, Texas, Georgia) are reducing the numbers of students per class, thereby increasing the need for more teachers. There are more students with special needs entering classrooms today, and schools need more teachers to assist those special needs students at all levels (Clement, 2000, p. 1). A trend that should not be overlooked is that of teacher attrition. Some studies show that as many as 50% of all new teachers leave the profession within the first five years of their career (Gordan, 1991; Haberman, 1995). Kantrowitz and Wingert (2000) reported a different kind of attrition, stating that many students who do graduate from teachers' colleges never set foot in classrooms to begin their careers (p. 38).

So, if many who major in a course that leads to teacher certification never teach, and half who enter the profession leave after a few short years, why should you be considering the profession? Is this a red flag for others who are trying to make the decision to teach? Or rather, should you be asking, "Why?" Why would someone major in education and then not teach? Why would someone leave the field during the first few years? What do they know that I don't?

Many people get jobs in fields that were not their major in college. Some students are still getting their teaching credentials to please their parents or counselors and going out into the world in a different profession. Some discover more lucrative positions with their major (especially in math or business) and simply decide not to teach.

The reasons for leaving the profession early in the career are varied, as well, but the problems faced by beginning teachers are real and documented (Dollase, 1992; Gordan, 1991; Veenman, 1984). The recurring problems of beginning teachers include classroom management and discipline, motivating students, dealing with students' problems, insufficient supplies and materials, dealing with special needs students, insufficient time to prepare, and working with parents, administrators, and the community (Clement, 2000, p. 69).

The challenges of teaching are real, but so are the opportunities. So much of surviving your first few years in the profession depends on your training, your attitude, and even your choice of where to begin your career. All of these will be discussed in other chapters.

WILL I GET A JOB?

The answer to "Will I get a job?" depends on you, your training and certification, your mastery of the knowledge base of teaching, your ability to interview well, and perhaps your willingness to move or commute to another area to gain experience. I personally know many graduates with teacher certification who work at the local bank, supermarket, and discount store. A teaching certificate does not guarantee you a teaching position, but it is certainly your best approach to entering the profession.

A SENSE OF MISSION OR CALLING

In 2000, Farkas, Johnson, and Foleno published *A Sense of Calling: Who Teaches and Why.* They report:

> [T]he newest cohort of teachers— those who have been in the classroom for five years or less . . . are highly motivated professionals who bring a strong sense of commitment and morale to their work. New teachers see themselves as talented, hardworking professionals who have responded to a calling. (p. 10)

Eighty-six percent of the teachers who participated in their research believed that "only those with 'a true sense of calling' should pursue the work [of teaching]" (p. 10).

Do you feel that your mission in life may be to help children, adolescents, or young adults? Have you had an experience working with youth that made you feel very fulfilled and needed? Did you have a teacher who was your role model and who encouraged you to become a teacher? Did you have a teacher who made everyone feel hurt, perhaps making you feel that you should become a teacher because you could certainly do a better job than he/she? These may be the strongest reasons to become a teacher. Many people choose teaching because they want to make a difference in the world. Christa McAuliffe, the first teacher representative on a space shuttle said, "I touch the future, I teach." Maybe you, too, want to change the world. If so, keep reading. If you want to be successful at teaching and changing the world, you have to get the best possible preparation to do so.

QUESTIONS/REFLECTIONS

1. Interview practicing teachers. Ask them why they chose teaching as a career. Ask about the biggest challenges faced in the classroom and the best rewards of the job. Try to interview someone who has taught less than three years and someone who has taught more than 15 years.

2. Go to one or more of the following Websites for more information about the current status of teachers, salaries, and the profession.
   www.aaee.org American Association for Employment in Education
   www.nea.org National Education Association
   www.aft.org American Federation of Teachers

3. Do a search to find your state's Department of Education on the Internet for a listing of job openings and salaries. Some school districts post this information on individual Websites.

CHAPTER 2

How Do I Become a Teacher?

There are multiple answers to the question, "How do I become a teacher?" The most general answer is to say that you can become a teacher by completing a teacher education program at an accredited college or university. This does not necessarily mean that you major in teacher education. Even the term "teacher education program" has a variety of meanings. The program itself may lead to teacher certification. However, to get teacher certification, you may have to do more than just complete the program. Why is this so complicated? Was it this complicated for all of your teachers to become teachers?

THE PUBLIC'S VIEW OF TEACHERS, ACCOUNTABILITY, AND STRICTER STANDARDS

My mother became an elementary school teacher during World War II by virtue of the fact that she had a high school diploma and was willing to take some summer courses. There was a real teacher shortage in the rural area where she lived and the county superintendent felt that anyone with a high school diploma could teach in a one-room school with a dozen children. Mother tells us that she survived well and enjoyed what she did during her two-year career. She taught just exactly as she had been taught, using the same books she had used in her own elementary experience. (Postscript: My dad came home from the Pacific campaign and my mom became a bride and left teaching.)

American education has changed dramatically since the late 1940s. Think about news stories you have seen or read about the public's perceptions of teachers and schools. Does the general public have respect for teachers and schools? Do you have respect for teachers and schools? Are there stories about ineffective schools? Are there schools that graduate students who can't read and write? Have you heard about teachers who have limited skills, even though they have college degrees? Have you heard that there is an 80% graduation rate nationwide and that in some states the high school graduation rate is only 60%? There are many negative stories in the media about the abysmal schools in existence and about the under-prepared teachers staffing those schools.

The result of public outcry over failing schools is often a call for better teachers. Teacher educators agree that every child in America should have "access to competent, caring, qualified teaching in schools organized for success" (National Commission on Teaching & America's Future, 1996, p. vi). The outcry for better teachers is one reason that it is more difficult to become a teacher today than in the past. As teaching has become more professional, professional organizations have raised their standards for those choosing to become teachers. Today's teachers are very accountable for what they do in their classrooms. Their students must pass standardized tests. In order to be accountable, teachers must be very well prepared.

PREPARATION IN A TRADITIONAL UNDERGRADUATE PROGRAM

The most common way to become a teacher remains the traditional undergraduate program. Even as a freshman entering a college or university, a student must decide what kind of teacher he/she intends to be before declaring a major or entering into a program. While every state and every university has different guidelines for teacher education students, there are some generalities. Each state has regulations for becoming a teacher, and every college and university that adheres to the standards set by their state is accredited for teacher education. The colleges and universities are reviewed annually or after a set number of years to maintain their accreditation to offer teacher education programs. Some colleges just meet the minimum state standards, while others far exceed them. So, if you hear that students at one university in your state have different requirements to become teachers than those at a nearby university, that is indeed possible. However, both will have the state's minimum standards embedded in their programs.

So, let's say you are a freshman and want to be a teacher. You probably can't just check a box and declare your major to be teaching. You will probably have to declare general studies until you meet the requirements for a teacher education program. Again, the requirements vary, but generally include completing two semesters of college with a certain grade-point average, the completion of an introduction to education course, an application to the teacher education program, and letters of recommendation from professors. Most people are very surprised that undergraduates can't just pick education as a major and that they have to earn a place in that program. Again, the public and the teaching profession have declared that they want only the best and the brightest in the programs.

Some states require a minimum ACT or SAT score before a student can enter a teacher education program. Georgia, for example, determined that students needed a 1,000 SAT or a 22 ACT to become teachers. If a student in Georgia does not have the minimum score, he/she can take a third test, called Praxis I to qualify to become a teacher.

ELEMENTARY EDUCATION MAJORS

What will you really major in? Before you declare this, you must make a decision about becoming a teacher of whom and of what. Do you want to teach elementary-aged students? If this is the case, you will probably major in EE—elementary education. In some states, this major is called early childhood education. Those who have majored in elementary education have generally been certified to teach in grades kindergarten through eighth. However, again, each state decides. In some states, elementary education majors finish with certifications to teach just first through sixth grades, or to teach pre-school through fifth. Teaching is becoming more specialized, and the programs that lead to certification reflect this.

In some states, early childhood education is a different option, and these programs prepare students to be certified teachers of preschool students, kindergarten, and early elementary grades. In some states, students who major in elementary education can only teach kindergarten through fifth grade and will need a special endorsement to teach younger children. If you know that your main interest is teaching in an elementary school, find out what this major is called in the college or university program you plan to enter and what grades this major will certify you to teach. How do you find out? Every college has a catalog with this information. Most colleges have their catalog online, and you can surf the Web to get this information. Your high school counselor will also have this information. Ask one of your own teachers, as they know what grades they can and can't teach.

MIDDLE SCHOOL MAJORS

If you thought that the choices and differences among existing programs in elementary education sounded confusing, the choices and differences in middle grades programs may seem even more convoluted. As a general rule, students can now major in middle grades education. This major leads to certification for teaching in grades four through eight, or nine, depending on the state. In some states the grades defined for middle grades may only be six through eight. It all depends on the state's requirements. So, if after taking your introduction to education class and meeting the requirements to be in a teacher education program, you have decided you want to teach in the middle grades, you can declare this as your major. As a middle grades major, you may be prepared to teach all subjects in these grades, or you may have to declare specializations, such as choosing areas from among language arts, social sciences, math, or science. In many states, middle grades majors are prepared to teach two areas for these grades.

Are there exceptions? Yes, there are. For example, some people who major in elementary education can also teach in the middle grades by taking a small number of extra courses. With these two or three extra courses, they can add what is called an endorsement to their teaching certificate. The same is true in some states where students can prepare to be high school teachers and qualify to teach in middle grades by adding a small number of courses. In some secondary programs, the student finishes the program eligible to teach his/her subject to students in high school and grades as low as sixth.

SECONDARY AND SPECIAL FIELDS

Unlike elementary and middle grades education, students wishing to become high school teachers and teachers of special fields such as art, music, and health and physical education will probably complete a major in their subject matter and add on the teacher education classes as a minor or as a "program." For example, if you want to be a high school math teacher, you may major in math and take a series of professional education courses that will constitute completion of the teacher education program. The same may be true for foreign languages, English, social studies, sciences, business, computer science, theater, and so forth. How many semester hours will be taken up by this series of professional education courses? Again, the answer varies widely from state to state, but an average might be a minimum of 30 semester hours.

Some colleges and universities differentiate between majoring in the subject matter itself and majoring in what they call teacher education for that subject matter. For example, I majored in Spanish education and not "pure" Spanish. I was not required to take quite as many hours of upper division Spanish classes in linguistics and literature as a "pure" Spanish major. By being freed from two or three classes, I was able to complete the teacher education sequence within my four years at the university. If you want to hear loud debates among professors of education, ask them if future teachers need to complete the same academic coursework as a major in that field who is pursuing teacher certification. Politicians now argue about this as well. No matter how you learn your subject matter, everyone agrees that you have to know your subject matter in order to teach it. Subject matter is also called your content field.

Music, art, and health and physical education have special rules, too. Often, to become a teacher in one of these fields, you will complete all of the courses for a major in the field, plus extra courses, plus the professional education courses. The end result is that when you finish one of these programs, you will probably be certified to teach the subject at all grade levels. So, if you major in music with teacher education, you can become a teacher of music for all grades, pre-school through high school. Some states differentiate between becoming a music or art teacher for elementary and secondary levels. You will certainly meet people who studied to become music teachers at the elementary level only, or at the high school level only. The same is true for health and physical education. What if you want to teach one of these subjects at a middle school? You have to find out which programs your state and university offer that include the middle school years. It can be included in an elementary or secondary program or both! If there is an overlap, then you must decide if you want to study to be an elementary teacher who teaches in the middle school program or a teacher who teaches middle grades and possibly teaches at the high school level, too. Remember, you may change your mind over the course of your teaching career, too.

SPECIAL EDUCATION, EDUCATION FOR EXCEPTIONAL CHILDREN, GIFTED, ESOL

Special education has many titles and a vocabulary all its own. Some schools and states refer to all special education teachers as teachers of exceptional children. These teachers have further subdivisions to their training and to their certification. For example, you may train to be a teacher of the visually or hearing impaired only, or of learning disabled students. Other specializations may include studying to be a teacher of children with behavior disorders. You may study to be a teacher of gifted children or a teacher of students who speak English as a Second Language (ESOL). With any of these areas, see the college catalog and find out if the college even offers the program in which you are interested. You may need to begin your search for a teacher education program in these areas by going to the Website for your state's Department of Education. If you are still in high school, your counselor can tell you which colleges and universities offer these programs.

For special education, you will major in that field. Your certification for the areas you teach will depend on the program you choose and your state's definition of grades to be taught. Studying to become a teacher of gifted children will probably mean that you finish a program for elementary education, middle grades education, or secondary education and then add on courses for the teaching of the gifted. Many teachers complete this add on after graduation. Some districts may pay for your add-on classes if you are already teaching. Others may give you a pay raise or a better class schedule if you complete additional coursework. The field of English as a Second Language is growing very rapidly and programs are added and changed almost annually in some institutions.

To summarize traditional undergraduate programs, we can say that there are many of them and that they vary greatly. Advisors of undergraduate students have often told them that if they are unsure of what to do with a major, that they should consider teacher education as a minor or as an add-on program. The truth is that in today's climate of teacher accountability, if students have not decided on becoming a teacher when they enter college, or at least by the end of their freshman year, they will be at the university for more than four years to complete their bachelor's degree. The idea that there is too much to learn about the subject matter and about how to teach in only four years has led many colleges and universities to develop fifth-year programs.

FIFTH-YEAR PROGRAMS

Since there is so much for undergraduates to learn in order to be prepared to be successful teachers, some programs became fifth-year programs by default. This means that while the student remains enrolled in a regular bachelor's program, he/she will probably need an extra semester or year to meet all requirements, including student teaching, unless the student opts to take overloaded semesters and summer school. Many college students now call themselves fifth-year seniors. For many students, the need to work at a paying job has meant that they must take lighter semesters and spread a four-year program into five years.

In some college programs, the catalog states clearly that teacher education will be a five-year bachelor's degree program. In these programs, the fifth year is dedicated exclusively to intensive teacher education courses, field experiences out in schools, and extended student teaching. The fifth year of the program may be yearlong student teaching in one or more schools or may be called an internship. While most fifth-year programs are designed as undergraduate ones, a few programs provide a master's at the end of the fifth (or sixth) year, or provide for some graduate credit to be earned while completing the bachelor's degree. What would be an advantage of staying a fifth year at your university? We know that the more preparation and experience a teacher education candidate receives, the better prepared he/she will be to go out and begin a teaching career. What is the downside? An extra year of college is very expensive, and while many college seniors get internships in the business world for pay, student teachers do not. In fact, student teachers pay full tuition for their experience.

POST-BACCALAUREATE PROGRAMS AND MASTER'S PROGRAMS IN EDUCATION

How many 18- and 19-year-olds in college really know what they want to major in while in their freshman or sophomore year? How many parents tell their children not to major in education because they won't make any money? In my orientation to education classes I ask, "What do your parents think of your decision to become a teacher?" The students' answers range from "It's okay with them" to "I think they are kind of worried" to even "They told me I'm too smart to be a teacher and should consider medicine or law."

When I advised post-baccalaureate teacher certification students in a previous job, many told me in their initial interviews that they had always wanted to be teachers, but that their parents and guidance counselors had advised them to get their bachelor's degrees in other fields and to choose other professions. These students had already earned a bachelor's degree and were now returning to our university to complete a teacher education program and earn their teacher certification. Referred to as "post-bacs" in higher education, these students each had an individualized program to take the undergraduate courses needed to complete their chosen program. It generally took two years as full-time students for them to complete their programs, and they did not receive a second bachelor's or a master's degree for their two years. They got their teaching credentials only. By the way, they paid graduate tuition to take undergraduate courses because they already had a bachelor's degree. As a word to the wise, if you are even considering teaching at all, it will take less time to major in an education program to begin with than to graduate with a degree in something else and then return to school for the teacher certification.

The variety of post-bac programs is as wide and varied as the variety of the previously discussed undergraduate programs. Some are as I described above, where students must have their undergraduate transcripts evaluated and then must take all courses not previously taken to complete a major in elementary education or middle grades or a major in the content field and the professional education courses for secondary teaching. Some states require stricter general education requirements for teacher education candidates than for those graduating in liberal arts and sciences, so a post-bac student can easily find himself/herself in a lower division (freshman/sophomore) course in history, political science, math, or science in order to meet teacher education guidelines. Some students have reported to me that they find this whole process to be demeaning and that it is certainly unfair to make someone with a bachelor's degree go back and take general education. However, is it fair to let someone be a teacher who hasn't taken what the undergraduates had to take to get their certification? The argument continues.

Some programs for teacher certification are at the master's level. Students take teacher certification courses at the graduate level, student teach, and receive a master's with teacher certification simultaneously. The big advantage with these programs is that a newly certified teacher with a master's degree will make more money than one with a bachelor's degree (up to $4,000 annually in some states). Arguments are made that someone who gets their teacher certification with a master's is certainly not a master's level teacher because they never took the bachelor's level work. Again, you will have to find out what is available in your state at colleges and universities.

THE ACCREDITATION OF YOUR CHOSEN COLLEGE OR UNIVERSITY

As already discussed, you cannot become a teacher at a college or university that does not offer teacher education programs in your chosen field. In addition to being accredited by the state, a college or university may apply for national certification in teacher education through NCATE, the National Council for Accreditation of Teacher Education. Only about half of all colleges and universities that prepare teachers nationwide earn this national accreditation. Why should you look at the NCATE accreditation when choosing your program? What other factors may tell you about the quality of the program? NCATE accreditation has been called the equivalent of a "good housekeeping seal of approval." It means that a team of experts visits the school at least every five years and checks the programs for quality. Every year follow-up reports are due. The faculty of NCATE schools must work together and discuss their programs and student progress through the programs. Very importantly, NCATE schools must prove that they have the resources to offer their programs and must prove that their graduates are able to pass state competency tests upon graduation. Some large state universities choose not to go through the rigors of applying for NCATE accreditation and insist that their universities have good enough reputations that they don't need another seal of approval. If you are considering a program at a college that does not have a national reputation, or a small private liberal arts school, you may want to consider looking at their NCATE status. You can get this information on the Website of the institution, or in their catalog, or simply by asking any faculty member in education.

ACTUAL CERTIFICATION VERSUS COMPLETING A PROGRAM

Does having this national accreditation mean that you can teach in any state if you complete a program? No, it does not. Getting your teacher certification means that you have completed the training for teacher certification, then passed a state competency test, and then applied for certification. Some people compare the competency test to passing state board exams in medicine or the bar exam in law. In many states, the application for certification will also ask you to sign a statement of ethics and submit to a criminal background check. Past felonies may prevent you from becoming a certified teacher even after completing a program and passing that final high-stakes competency test. In most introduction to education classes, students are counseled about which offenses will not permit them to become certified. In Georgia, for example, any student who has been arrested for DUI will have to submit paperwork about that offense to the state board before consideration for certification. While one DUI will probably not keep you from becoming a teacher, it is always better to know that these questions will be asked at the end of a program before you complete two to four years of study in the major.

Do some students complete programs and then fail to pass the final state competency tests? Yes, this happens routinely. Ask about your chosen college's pass rates before you make the decision to attend. Remember, just taking a class does not mean that you have learned all the material needed to teach. You have to really learn the material and you have to reflect on your learning to feel confident about both your content knowledge and your ability to teach the material. Depending on your state, you may be tested on both your knowledge of the subject and your knowledge about how to teach.

CERTIFICATION IN ANOTHER STATE

Your teacher certification, whether gained through an alternative route or a traditional route, is only good in the state issuing the certification. Once certified in your state, you may apply for certification in another state. Some states have reciprocal agreements and the only thing that you will have to do is apply for certification and submit proof of your initial certification. There will most probably be a processing fee. Without reciprocal agreements, you may have to take another standardized competency test that has been developed by that state. Some states will require a copy of all transcripts and will evaluate your coursework as compared to theirs. You may then need to take some courses and pass their test. Each state is different. See the listing of state teacher certification offices provided in the appendix to this book and begin your search for information about each state's requirements there.

ALTERNATIVE ROUTES TO CERTIFICATION

You may know people who never majored in education or completed a minor or teacher education program but who became teachers. In times of high teacher demand, some states approve alternative routes to certification. Some urban cities get special permission from their state departments to hire noncertified teachers to simply fill vacant positions. What is alternative certification and is it a good idea for you?

Alternative certification may mean allowing people with some credentials to teach for a limited amount of time until they complete full certification. An alternative route can mean that the student takes a minimum number of courses and then teaches under the guidance of a mentor or other outside observer. Georgia is one state that has some alternative routes to certification, due to teacher shortages in high demand areas such as math, science, foreign language, and middle grades.

Someone with a bachelor's degree in a high-need field who takes and passes the state's standardized competency test for teachers in that field (Praxis II) may apply for a provisional certificate and may then be hired as a full-time teacher. While teaching, the person must complete a series of classes taught by colleges, universities, and/or the regional offices of education. In addition, the teacher must be supervised regularly by a college or regional office of education, and they must be assigned a mentor teacher in the district. They have approximately two years to complete their program and then apply for regular certification. They are generally paid somewhat less than a fully certified teacher.

The advantages of this program are that people who know their subject matter are getting into classrooms where they are needed. However, if a teacher has not had any formal training in how to teach, manage a classroom, and deal with today's students, he/she may become totally overwhelmed and completely ineffective in the classroom. A newly hired teacher with no training may suffer such stress that they are not effective in the classroom. Sometimes, teachers' unions are opposed to provisionally certified people working in schools and may fight against that person being there. The added time constraints of having to attend classes two nights or more a week may be very difficult for the new hire.

In other programs, students who already have a bachelor's degree may take all the coursework for teacher certification, then get a job before student teaching. The advantage for these students is that instead of paying more tuition, they are being paid, although generally less than a certified teacher. The disadvantage is that they have missed what many students tell us is the most beneficial part of their program, student teaching.

Yes, there are teacher shortages in some parts of the country and yes, subject matter specialists are needed to teach in high demand fields. Some states are willing to risk placing provisionally certified people in schools to meet the demands of the shortages. Some alternative routes to certification may be more rigorous than others, so you will have to investigate before you choose a program, if this is your interest. Advocates of alternative routes to certification claim that the demand for teachers forces them to offer these programs and the programs can be of high quality. Proponents say that there are no shortcuts to becoming a teacher and that someone who is not fully prepared will not be as effective as one who is prepared. Teaching still struggles with gaining the professionalism of law and medicine, fields that have few, if any, alternatives and shortcuts to certification.

TEACHING WITHOUT A CERTIFICATE

Yes, some schools will indeed hire you without a teaching certificate. Some private schools feel that your subject matter background may be the most important factor in your qualifications. Remember, too, that the majority of community colleges, colleges, and universities hire faculty for their content knowledge and do not require teaching credentials.

While some private schools will hire teachers without teacher certification, they may then require that teacher to earn certification within a limited amount of time. Other schools may set a date by which all teachers must earn certification because the school itself wants to upgrade its accreditation. The parents who send their children to a private school may start the required teacher certification movement. It may be a risk to your job security not to be certified, even in a school that does not initially require it. On the other hand, gaining the experience in the classroom may show you if you really do want to spend years of life back in college earning teacher certification.

SUBSTITUTE TEACHING

Most people who work in education think that substitute teachers deserve gold stars and a special place in heaven for their work. Their jobs have no security and are often completed under the worst of circumstances. Their phone rings and they may have only minutes to get organized and begin their day—without any previous knowledge of their students and the curriculum.

How do you become a substitute teacher? Again, each state has its own set of guidelines and regulations. In many states, substitutes must have a bachelor's degree, take a minimum amount of staff development training in the school district or a regional office of education, and apply for a substitute teaching certificate. This application probably carries with it a criminal background check. A few states require only a high school diploma, the staff development training, and a completed application. Some private schools may only require an interview with the principal. A fully certified teacher can generally substitute by simply presenting proof of certification to the district or regional office. Some districts will pay a substitute more money if they are a fully certified teacher. In areas where there are not shortages of teachers, certified teachers have often found that they must work as substitutes for one or more years in order to "get their foot in the door" for permanent employment.

Some people choose to be substitutes because of the flexibility it allows them. If you are interested in working only three days a week, you can be a substitute and pick your schedule. Principals know their good substitutes and would know that you are only available Mondays, Tuesdays, and Thursdays. Others choose subbing because it does not involve the extra-curricular duties and time commitments that full-time teaching does. You generally get to leave school without papers to grade or plans to write, and if the class's standardized test scores are low, the substitute is not the teacher held accountable for that.

The downside of subbing is that you have to find a way to manage and control students that you generally do not know. The regular teacher may not have left plans and even first graders have been known to say, "you're not a real teacher and we're not going to do what you say." It is hard to adjust to a different room and a different school every day or every week. Yes, you do have to keep students busy and on-task, which may mean doing some lesson planning and reading and studying after school hours. There won't be health insurance benefits or retirement credits for substitute teachers.

QUESTIONS/REFLECTIONS

1. Find an article in a recent magazine or newspaper about teachers and the profession of teaching. Is it positive or negative? What does it say about the public's perception of teachers and their jobs?

2. Interview a substitute teacher. Why does he/she choose to be a substitute? What are the biggest challenges in subbing? What are the rewards?

3. Talk with a teacher who began his/her career without student teaching or completing a traditional teacher education program. What does this teacher say about the challenges and stresses of the early years of teaching? Are this teacher's answers to your questions any different from the answers of a teacher who went through a traditional program to teach?

4. Choose a state other than your own and find out what you would have to do to become certified to teach there. Use the Internet to search for the information. Is the information available or will you have to call to find out what the requirements are?

5. Divide your class or group in half and have each side debate the pros and cons of alternative routes to certification. What alternative routes are available in your state? Should there be other/ better alternatives?

6. Take the role of parents who send their child to school. Who do you want to teach your children? What type of training and certification do you want those teachers who work with your children to have?

CHAPTER 3

What Do I Have to Learn to Be a Teacher?

On her end-of-the-semester course evaluation, one of the freshmen in my orientation to education wrote, "Until I took this course, I never knew that there was so much to learn to become a teacher. I just thought 'What's to learn?' I already know how to read and I certainly know more math, science, and social studies than the second graders I plan to teach." This is perhaps not atypical of what the general public thinks about the level of skills needed to teach. The truth is that there is indeed a knowledge base for the profession of teaching and that learning to teach is a discipline to be mastered.

ORIENTATION OR INTRODUCTION TO EDUCATION

Called orientation to education in some colleges and introduction to education in others, this course may vary in length from a series of seminars that give no credit hours to a three-semester-hour course. The goals of the first course in the education sequence are to acquaint students with state and college guidelines for teacher education, familiarize students with the realities of today's students, classrooms, and schools, and to introduce students to the vocabulary of the teaching profession. Most introductory courses cover how schools are governed, some history of education, and an introduction to the current hot topics and reform movements in education. Teacher salaries, the professionalism of teaching, the status of today's children, tips for finding a first job, and what the first year of teaching is like are all topics for the introductory course. An introductory class will probably cover the steps for progressing through the teacher education program and how to qualify for teacher certification in the state.

Some introductory classes focus on the history and foundations of education more than anything else. Professors of these courses feel that you can't work in a system whose history you do not understand. Other courses focus more on letting students explore their personal histories with teachers and their decision to pursue a teacher education program.

Some orientation courses require field experiences, meaning that in addition to the time spent in the classroom on campus, students will be required to spend time in a school observing students and talking with teachers. If the course has a field experience component, find out early how the experience is arranged. Will you have to find your placement in a school or will you be assigned to a designated teacher? How many hours will you be expected to fulfill in that classroom and what will you have to do while there? You may have to get liability insurance before going out into a school to be an observer and you may have to submit to fingerprinting and a criminal background check before going out to your field experience. (See the section in this chapter on field experience.) Why? Today's schools are much more conscious than ever before about the problems of violence and criminal trespass in their buildings. Schools are required to do everything in their power to protect their students and that includes keeping strangers out.

In the introductory course you may be asked to apply for admission to teacher education and provide proof of successful completion of a general skills test or a certain level of achievement on the ACT or SAT test. In essence, the orientation and introductory courses serve two functions: recruitment of prospective students into teacher education and screening for the best qualified prospective students. For more about the content of introductory courses, read some sample textbooks used in those courses. See, for example, Wiseman, Cooner, and Knight's *Becoming a Teacher in a Field-Based Setting*; Armstrong, Henson, and Savage's *Teaching Today*; Parkay and Hardcastle Stanford's *Becoming a Teacher*; Ryan and Cooper's *Those Who Can, Teach*; Travers and Rebore's *Foundations of Education*; and Morrison's *Teaching in America*.

Some programs may require a history and philosophy of education course in addition to introduction to education. This history and philosophy course may be the second course in your teacher education program, or it may be a course at the end of your requirements. Some programs do not require separate courses for each strand of the knowledge base, but rather they combine courses, offering, for example, courses called "Teaching I" and "Teaching II" that cover the topics of a traditional introductory course, a history and philosophy or foundations course, and an educational psychology course.

EDUCATIONAL PSYCHOLOGY

How do you learn best? How do students learn? How can you reach all the students in your classroom and motivate each to excel? What kinds of rewards motivate third graders? What will motivate a middle school student? Will a behaviorist learning theory work better with some students than others? Why or why not? Should you be a constructivist teacher? Why do principals insist that the curriculum be developmentally appropriate? What does developmentally appropriate mean? These are all questions that are typically addressed in educational psychology. As Henson and Eller (1999, p. xvii) write, "By helping teachers understand why students behave as they do, educational psychology . . . can prepare teachers to analyze situations and make appropriate choices." Some say that the study of psychology is truly the basis of the study of how to be an effective teacher, because so much of teaching is communication and dealing with "real" children with "real" issues and problems.

Some education programs will require students to take an introduction to psychology course and a course in child or developmental psychology before the course in educational psychology. An introductory course in psychology better prepares the student for the specific topics covered in educational psychology. A large part of the course will be studying how students develop—emotionally, morally, socially, cognitively, and in their development of language. You will then study how the differences among students affect your teaching. For example, how can you teach students who do not speak English as a native language? What do you need to know about students with attention deficit disorder so that you can teach them?

In educational psychology you learn about learning theories and what motivates students to learn best. You will learn about managing student behavior and the advantages and disadvantages of creating systems of rewards and consequences in your classroom. In some educational psychology classes you study assessment and learn how to evaluate and grade your students. These are all important skills for succeeding in the classroom.

CURRICULUM

The most general definition of curriculum is "what is taught in the schools." When asked about their curriculum, some teachers say that the curriculum is the guide for what material they have to cover in a given grade and subject area. Many teachers cite the topics in their textbooks and supplemental materials as the curriculum that they teach. Wiles and Bondi (1998, p. 31) define curriculum as "a plan for learning," saying that this plan should "contain a vision of what should be, as well as a structure that translates those visions into experiences for learning."

A typical undergraduate class in curriculum begins with teaching students about the national and state standards for their subject matter. While there is no national curriculum for each subject taught, there are professional associations that have created guidelines for their subject content. For example, the National Council for the Teaching of Mathematics (NCTM) has published standards regarding the teaching of math, the American Council for the Teaching of Foreign Languages (ACTFL) has published their standards for foreign languages, and the National Council of Teachers of English (NCTE) for English. Each state of the United States has its own set of curriculum standards for each grade and subject level. Furthermore, many individual districts take the standards of the national associations and their state's standards to create a set of district standards, which are published as curriculum guidelines. If this sounds complicated, think for a moment about two third graders in different classrooms in the same district. Should they be learning the same material in a school year? Should third graders in two schools in different cities of the state be learning the same things? These questions should get answered in a curriculum class.

Once the general guidelines of what should be taught are covered, then students learn about how to choose a textbook, how to use that textbook, and how to supplement the textbook to make lessons interesting. There are major differences in textbooks, and while many teachers begin their careers worrying about how to get through the book in a year, veteran teachers know that many of the lessons that they teach will not come from the book at all.

In curriculum classes students learn how to write lesson plans. Lesson plans are not just laundry lists that say which pages of the book are to be covered on which days, but are maps of what the teacher and the students will do to learn the material (the curriculum). A good lesson plan has goals to guide the teacher, objectives for what the students will learn and be able to do, a variety of presentations and activities, and an assessment of student learning. Let's be very realistic here. If you were to be given the responsibility for teaching 26 fourth graders tomorrow from 8 A.M. until 3:15 P.M., wouldn't you want a good plan to follow to help you teach these students? You are not only responsible for keeping these children out of trouble and busy, but they must *learn* something, too. Imagine that you have been hired to teach five 50-minute classes, each with 30 high school students, and you are responsible for teaching them enough science to do well on their college entrance ACT or SAT exams. Do you want to know what to teach, which books to choose, and how to plan for each week? This is what you learn in curriculum.

Curriculum classes are also where you learn how to make long-range plans for units and semesters. You learn how to assess student learning, which means learning how to write tests, how to grade papers, and how to help students reflect on their own progress. You should learn how to set up appropriate grading scales and how to assess work without the use of traditional grades.

METHODS COURSES

Curriculum and methods are so closely tied that they are often taught in one class. As you learn what to teach, you will then learn how to teach that curriculum. For secondary majors, there may be a general curriculum and methods course, followed by a course in the teaching of the subject, such as English methods, math methods, methods of teaching sciences, or methods of teaching social studies. What's the difference? If you plan to be a science teacher, you need to know how to write lesson plans, how to write unit plans, and how to grade students. In addition, you need to know about the use of labs in the teaching of science, how to teach the scientific method, and how to integrate some of your courses with those of the math department.

For elementary education majors, there will be a series of courses for curriculum and methods in each of the subject fields. You must know about the teaching of sciences, math, language arts, and social studies. Elementary majors will have courses devoted to the teaching of reading, since so much of the early years of school are devoted to reading.

You will also be expected to take courses about health, physical educa-tion, art, and music, because in some schools the elementary teacher still teaches everything, without the help of specialists.

Methods courses can, and should be, very hands-on courses for the students. You should be learning how to teach by doing activities that you will then use in your classes. By the time you are in methods courses, you should also be spending quite a bit of time out in the schools, where you will be paired with a practicing classroom teacher and will have the opportunity to practice teaching lessons.

What kinds of methods will you learn? You will learn how to ask good questions, not just questions that require yes/no answers. You will learn how to teach concepts and how to give clear presentations/lec-tures to your students. You will learn about mastery learning, about when and how to group students, and about how to use demonstrations and role plays in your classroom. A methods course will teach you how to use media in your classroom—computers, videos, CDs, and the Internet—and how to integrate media with the textbook. Your methods class will help you to hone your planning and assessment skills.

What's to learn? There is so much to learn because teaching is both an art and a science. You may have been in classes with teachers who just seemed like they were born to teach. Maybe they were born to teach, or maybe they learned the hard way, through trial and error. Perhaps they were fortunate enough to have attended a college with good methods classes. For a better idea of what is taught in curriculum and methods classes, see, for example, the following textbooks: Kellough and Kel-lough's *Secondary School Teaching: A Guide to Methods and Resources*; Cruikshank, Bainer, and Metcalf's *The Act of Teaching*; McNeil's *Cur-riculum: The Teacher's Initiative*; Moore's *Classroom Teaching Skills*; Or-lich et al.'s *Teaching Strategies: A Guide to Better Instruction*; and Schurr, Thomason, and Thomason's *Teaching at the Middle Level*.

EXCEPTIONAL CHILDREN, SPECIAL EDUCATION, AND GIFTED EDUCATION

Most teacher education programs now require at least one course in the education and psychology of exceptional children. Often called the spe-cial ed course, this course deals with learning how to diagnose the spe-cial needs of children, how to make adaptations and modifications to your lesson plans for special needs students, and how to assess their learning. The special needs may be behavioral in nature or may be related to learning patterns. Obviously, as a teacher you need to know how to work with students who have learning disabilities. These students may have sight or hearing problems, problems with dyslexia, attention deficit disorder, or a myriad of other learning difficulties. New research on "crack babies" and other children born to addicted or alcoholic parents is now starting to be included in courses on exceptional children.

Do not forget that gifted students will also need special attention in your classroom. Susan Winebrenner (1992, p. 1) writes, "It may surprise you to find that in a class that has a range of abilities (and which class doesn't?), it is the most able, rather than the least able, who will learn less new material than any other group." So, your special ed class should include units that will help you to assist the exceptionally gifted and talented students in your room as well.

While you will learn to modify your lesson plans and make adaptations in your classroom for students with special needs and gifted students, you should also learn how to work with specialist teachers who may have programs for your students. While many special needs students today are mainstreamed into the "regular" or traditional classroom, they may still be pulled out for tutoring with specialist teachers. In some cases the specialist comes to your room and works with the student while you are teaching the whole class. The same is true for gifted students. Learning what the specialist teachers do will help you to meet the needs of all students. Some recent graduates report that they learned what should happen in successful special education programs while in college, but found that the real world was simply not operating that way. For this reason, your special education class will probably also have a field experience attached to it. In your field experience you may be asked to observe and monitor special needs students in a classroom, tutor students, or interview both regular and specialist teachers about the specifics of their programs to meet the needs of all students. This class will probably include a section on school law as it pertains to meeting the needs of all children and may include a section on child abuse and your responsibilities as a teacher in reporting cases of abuse.

CLASSROOM MANAGEMENT

When I was in college studying to be a teacher, my professors said that if we wrote good lesson plans and kept students busy, that we would never have to worry about classroom management and discipline. The field of study and the knowledge base about classroom management and discipline has increased 100% in the past 20 years. We now know that as many as half of all beginning teachers leave the profession within the first five years, and we know that dealing with students' problems and managing the students' behavior is a contributing factor to the teacher dropout rate. We also have a tremendous amount of research-based knowledge on which to build positive classroom management plans. Unlike my former professors, I tell student teachers that they must first have a classroom management plan that works, then they can get to teach their lesson plan.

So, you should take a course in classroom management that is both theoretical and practical. By reading books such as Charles's *Building Classroom Discipline*, Tauber's *Classroom Management: Theory and Practice*, and Burden's *Classroom Management and Discipline*, you will become aware of the reasons that your students misbehave and the history of what teachers have tried for discipline in the past.

Since classroom management varies widely by grade levels, your class should have readings that are specific to your level of teaching. Books such as Weinstein and Mignano's *Elementary Classroom Management*, Canter and Canter's *Behavior Management in the Middle School Classroom*, and Weinstein's *Secondary Classroom Management* are designed for the specific needs of those grade levels.

With regard to classroom management, you need to know that how you set up your classroom and how you set the tone for the first day of school are crucial factors for your success or failure with your class. Until you are a respected veteran with a reputation for no nonsense in your room, you need to work on becoming established as one. A large component of becoming established includes creating a management plan with rules, consequences, and positives. For help with becoming established, you will read books such as Wong and Wong's *The First Days of School* and Canter and Canter's *Succeeding with Difficult Students* and *Assertive Discipline*.

In a management course you should learn strategies for defusing dangerous situations such as fights, and should role-play how you will talk to students in confrontations. You will learn that your voice, your eyes, and your body posture are very important components of classroom management. Of course, you will learn that what you teach students does have to be well organized and clearly presented to keep students busy and on-task, so the old professors who used to say that a good lesson plan was the best plan for classroom management weren't all wrong.

In an effective classroom management course you will also learn about communicating with parents, since parents are very important partners with you as you teach your students. You should learn about how and when to call parents, ways to conduct productive conferences, and when to write newsletters home.

Classroom management is a very important component of successful teaching and a required course in management should help you feel prepared for your student teaching experience.

FIELD EXPERIENCES AND STUDENT TEACHING

Before the late 1970s, student teachers often completed all of their coursework on the college campus and then went to a school for eight weeks or a semester of student teaching. Many student teachers discovered that the real world of teaching was not for them, graduated with teaching credentials, but never taught. Since the late 1970s most teacher education programs have included field experiences before student teaching. Called practicum experiences or early field experiences at some colleges, they are designed for the college student to understand the realities of today's classrooms well before the in-depth student teaching experience.

Most of your teacher education classes will have a field experience component. You may be required to be on campus fewer hours per week for a class, then be expected to be in a school for the remainder of the hours. In some classes, you will meet on campus and be expected to complete a certain number of hours off campus in a school for no college credit. The rationale for this is that your field experience leads to teacher certification, not college credit. Yet another model for field experience is that your college class and its professor will meet in a school every week during the semester, and you will immediately leave your class to spend time in a teacher's classroom.

Many programs require about 100 clock hours of early field experience before student teaching. A course in curriculum may carry with it 30 required hours in a school. Your methods class may require another 30, your management class 15, your exceptional child class 15, and your introduction to education class 10. What do you actually do in field experience? This varies depending upon your professor, but most students begin by observing the teacher. This observation should be active. For example, you may be asked to write a lesson plan of what the teacher is doing, while he/she is teaching. After the lesson ends, you will want to interview the teacher and discuss how he/she planned the lesson, finding out if the goals and objectives on the original plan were met. You may observe individual students and chart their behavior and the teacher's responses to them. Does the teacher call on boys and girls evenly? Did he/she teach directly from a textbook or were additional resources used? How did the teacher assess the students' learning?

After you have observed for a while, you will probably be asked to teach a short lesson or to teach a small group of students. This is good practice for you to prepare for student teaching. Sometimes you will be asked to grade papers or to assist the teacher in writing or copying tests. Again, this is all good practice. In some college classes, you will be required to teach several lessons, totaling three or four hours of whole-class teaching and your college professor will observe one of the lessons for a grade. You may be evaluated by the classroom teacher and his/her evaluation will be used to determine if you qualify for student teaching. So, field experiences are very important. I once worked with a college student who became so nervous before teaching her lesson to a small group of students in her field experience that she would faint. By discovering this in field experience, she was counseled out of teacher education into another major. It was a much better situation than having her complete three and a half years of college in teacher education and then discover through student teaching that this was not her field.

Student teaching still varies in length from one semester to year-long experiences. During student teaching you may be assigned to one teacher for the entire time, or your assignment may be split between two teachers. During most of your student teaching you are expected to work the same hours as your assigned teacher, who is called the cooperating teacher. If the school requires its teachers to be there from 7:30 to 3:30, then those are your hours. Do not expect a long lunch hour, as most teachers are lucky to have half an hour for lunch. You probably will not be able to run errands or go to the grocery store over lunch — you will be busy planning and preparing and maybe even working with the students. Also, be sure to turn off your cell phone when you student teach, as you cannot take personal calls while teaching a classroom of students. In fact, some school have rules prohibiting teachers from carrying cell phones to work. As a student teacher, you need to follow the rules that apply to the regular teachers, and you need to dress professionally. You need to look more like a teacher than a student, and dressing like a teacher is the first step toward being accepted as one.

Do you get paid for all the work you do as a student teacher? No, you pay full tuition for working as a student teacher. Your tuition is used to pay your college supervisor and to sometimes pay your cooperating teacher. The classroom teacher sometimes gets paid a stipend for accepting a student teacher, such as $50 for the semester. Some colleges pay $200 to $300 to the cooperating teachers for their work. At some universities, the cooperating teachers get no payment, but may choose to take a class without paying tuition. Why do teachers accept student teachers? The answer is not money, since the payments are generally very low. Some teachers report that they like the free tuition, but most tell us that they simply want to help a new teacher get started. The idea of mentoring a student teacher appeals to many veteran teachers, and they like the opportunity to learn some new ideas from a new graduate. Unfortunately, some teachers do take advantage of the student teachers and accept them into their classroom as free labor. The best student teaching assignments are ones where the cooperating teacher and the student teacher work collaboratively and become team teachers.

Will you get to pick your cooperating teacher and school? Probably not. Most universities must rely upon nearby school districts and send the list of student teachers to personnel directors or principals who pair the student teachers with their cooperating teachers. In some cases you may request that a teacher you met in your field experience be your cooperating teacher, but there are no guarantees. Some colleges require that the cooperating teachers have a master's degree, a minimum number of years of experience, and special training in order to supervise the student teacher. Because of the need for schools to be within driving distance of campus, some colleges are not as strict in their requirements of the cooperating teacher. You should not expect to student teach where you went to school or in a school where your own children are in attendance.

What will you actually do in student teaching? You will observe how your teacher plans, organizes, and delivers lessons, then you will begin to teach the classes yourself. Be prepared to help out with extra duties, such as lunch supervision and bus duties, because your student teaching experience is supposed to be as much like real teaching as possible, and real teachers have many extra duties. Hopefully you will be able to develop your classroom management skills during student teaching, as well as your skills in presenting lessons and assessing students. You should leave student teaching with both confidence and concrete ideas.

YOUR LIABILITY AS A PRACTICUM STUDENT AND STUDENT TEACHER

Most practicing teachers carry professional liability insurance. This insurance provides protection if they are sued by the parents of students that they are teaching. Why are teachers sued? Teachers are sometimes sued because students do not learn in their classes. Some teachers have been sued because they have not promoted students to another grade or because students have not learned to read in their classes. Teachers are also sued if students are hurt or injured while in their classes. As a teacher, you may be open to litigation if a fight breaks out in your room or on the playground when you are supervising that area. You may be sued for touching a student inappropriately or for negligence in protecting a student from being teased and insulted by other students. You may be open to a lawsuit for failure to report suspected child abuse or for reporting suspected abuse that turns out not to be.

As a student teacher, or even as a field experience student, parents consider you a responsible adult in their child's classroom. If there is a problem or crisis and the parents consider a suit against the classroom teacher, you may also be named because you are an adult in that classroom. To protect yourself, you will want to consider professional liability insurance. In fact, most colleges and universities will require you to obtain such insurance, or waive your right to do so, before allowing you to go out into a school. Most students get professional liability insurance from the National Education Association (NEA), the American Federation of Teachers (AFT), or a state teachers' association. The good news about this type of insurance is that if you join one of these associations as a student, your dues will be very low and will include the liability insurance. In 2001, college students could join the NEA for as little as $10 a year in some states. Some students still object to joining a "union" and therefore do not get insurance through the NEA or AFT. You can purchase an individual policy for liability insurance through many insurance companies. This insurance does not prevent people from suing you, but rather this insurance exists to help pay the cost of legal fees in the event that you are taken into court and sued.

In addition to obtaining liability insurance, you will probably have to submit to a criminal background check and fingerprinting before going out into the schools for field experiences and student teaching.

DIVERSITY OF FIELD EXPERIENCES

Some states not only mandate the total hours required in field experiences and student teaching, but also mandate the grade levels of students with whom you must have field experience. For example, if you are studying to be an elementary teacher, you may have to prove that you have worked with very young children at the preschool level, children that are in grades two through three, and students in grades four through five to be eligible for certification. Your college should track your experiences in order for you to qualify for certification at the end of your teacher education program.

Your state, or your college program, may also require that your field experiences include work with students of diverse backgrounds. For example, you may need to complete a field experience in a school with few minority students and an experience in a school with a minimum of 30% minority students. You may be required to complete an experience in a school with language minority children. Again, each state varies its requirements, as does each university. The general rule is the more field experience, the better prepared you will be.

QUESTIONS/REFLECTIONS

1. Get a college catalog and review the required courses for your teacher education program. (Remember, most catalogs are now available on-line, too.) How many courses in curriculum and methods are required? How many field experiences are attached to your required courses? Is there a course in classroom management or a separate course in assessment and grading of students?

2. Get an advisement sheet from your college's teacher education department. How can all of the required courses be fit into your four years of college if you are an undergraduate student? If you are pursuing teacher certification with a master's degree or as a graduate student, how long will this program take? When do the courses meet and can you take these courses while still working full- or part-time?

CHAPTER 4

Today's Students and Their Diversity

In the orientation to education class that I teach, my students complete a unit about at-risk students. At-risk students are any students who may be at risk of failing a class, dropping out of school before high school graduation, or at risk of simply not succeeding at some aspect of school. Some teachers call their at-risk students the ones who "fall through the cracks" of the school and do not receive the help they need. My students read about the effects of poverty, race/ethnicity, and gender on a student's chances of succeeding in school. They study demographics, school violence, child abuse, gang activity, and changes in family lifestyles and how these factors influence today's children. The unit ends with some scary statistics about teenage pregnancy, nutritional deficits, and drug abuse. After the last set of statistics is discussed, I say to students, "You now know the tough odds that some of your future students face. How will you take these at-risk students who come into your classroom and turn them into at-promise students?" This question does not have any easy answers, but the courses offered in multicultural education and diversity may help future teachers begin to grapple with how to educate all students, especially those who are at risk.

MULTICULTURAL EDUCATION

Today's students certainly mirror today's population and our population is becoming increasingly diverse. What does the increase in diversity mean for today's classrooms? The students in our classes are from a myriad of economic, cultural, and ethnic backgrounds, as well as from homes where English is not the family's first language. The first goal of a new teacher must be acceptance of all students who enter the door to the classroom. It is especially important that new teachers gain experiences working with diverse students before accepting their first teaching assignment. The field of multicultural education has emerged to help prepare teachers to effectively teach the populations they will encounter.

Duarte and Smith (2000) summarize the goals for multicultural education with the following:

> National standards documents, curriculum materials, and scholarly treatises extolling the goals of multicultural education abound. In these materials, educators are encouraged to respect the diverse perspectives of their students, to promote understanding between students from various cultural groups, and to ensure that students from all cultural backgrounds are guaranteed equal educational opportunities. (p. vii)

Sonia Nieto's (2000) definition of multicultural education is based in a sociopolitical context:

> Multicultural education is a process of comprehensive school reform and basic education for all students. It challenges and rejects racism and other forms of discrimination in schools and society and accepts and affirms the pluralism (ethnic, racial, linguistic, religious, economic, and gender, among others) that students, their communities, and teachers reflect. Multicultural education permeates the schools' curriculum and instructional strategies, as well as the interactions among teachers, students, and families, and the very way that schools conceptualize the nature of teaching and learning. Because it uses critical pedagogy as its underlying philosophy and focuses on knowledge, reflection, and action (praxis) as the basis for social change, multicultural education promotes democratic principles of social justice.

The seven basic characteristics of multicultural education in this definition are:

> Multicultural education is antiracist education.
> Multicultural education is basic education.
> Multicultural education is important for all students.
> Multicultural education is pervasive.
> Multicultural education is education for social justice.
> Multicultural education is a process.
> Multicultural education is critical pedagogy. (p. 305)

Your college or university may require a course in multicultural education that presents the history and philosophy of the multicultural education movement. Your required course may have a different focus, such as how to implement strategies that lead to acceptance and tolerance of all students, or how to better educate immigrant children who are entering today's schools. For examples of texts about strategies and immigrant children, see Igoa's *The Inner World of the Immigrant Child* and Davidman and Davidman's *Teaching with a Multicultural Perspective*.

The most practical, bottom line on multicultural education is that today's teachers should not expect to teach in classrooms where the student body looks like it did when they were students. New teachers need to be prepared to accept all students, to find ways to teach all students the required curriculum, and, in addition, to teach tolerance and acceptance to their students. These are not small tasks and one course in this area is just a beginning to being successful in this area.

A COLLEGE COURSE IN DIVERSITY

The college where I teach recently implemented a new required course in diversity for teacher education majors. Called "Explorations in a Diverse Culture," this course is designed to give students experiences in another culture where they are a minority and where they do not speak the language of the majority of the population. This course will be offered every May and will only be offered off-campus. For example, students may choose to study in Costa Rica or Mexico, where they will participate in Spanish classes, anthropology classes, and visit schools for field experience. Other sections of the course will be offered in New York City, Atlanta, and school districts such as Dalton, Georgia, that have extremely high populations of non–English-speaking immigrant students. It is hoped that these immersion classes will help to promote acceptance and tolerance on the part of the teachers, as well as give them some insights into teaching language-minority children.

ESOL

ESOL refers to teaching English to Speakers of Other Languages. This field has developed because so many students in today's classrooms are not native speakers of English, and most teacher education programs will have a unit about teaching ESOL in a curriculum and methods course. Some colleges will have one or more required courses in ESOL for all majors. Why would all majors be required to have knowledge and understanding of how to teach students who do not speak English as a native language? The answer is because these students are in all of our classes—mathematics, science, English, physical education, social studies, vocational classes, music—everything.

ESOL is different from a foreign language classroom. When you have non–English-speaking students in your classes, they will not all speak the same languages. While some people advocated that new teachers should take as much Spanish as possible, it must be noted that Spanish is only one foreign language and that your students may speak Asian languages, eastern European languages, Portuguese, French, or Central American Indian dialects as native languages. The areas of the country where ESOL is needed continues to grow, so these classes are not just needed in Texas, California, Florida, and Georgia.

What do you learn in an ESOL class? You will learn some basic linguistics in this class. You will also learn about culture and how to be accepting of the many cultures of the students who come into your classroom. You will learn methods of teaching your subject matter so that students with limited English proficiency can learn the content of your course and learn English at the same time. For example, when teaching a class with students with limited English, you quickly learn to always use visual clues for the students. Even if you are just announcing what page the students should open their books to, you should write that number on the board so that all students understand.

An ESOL course will teach you strategies for reaching your students and will teach you about working with the ESOL specialists who may be assigned to your building. Team teaching with an ESOL teacher requires special skills and much advance organization. This course should also help you with how to prepare students with limited English proficiency for standardized tests. When I have discussed the issue of standards and accountability with my orientation classes, they were very surprised to learn that their students with limited English will still take the same standardized tests that their English-speaking students will take. Imagine the stress caused if you are a fifth-grade teacher with a class where 50% of your students are not native English speakers and your class's test scores will be compared to the other fifth grades across the district and state. If the other classes have only English-speaking students, and the test is in English, one would certainly expect their test scores to be higher. This is not a hypothetical situation. It happens every spring during standardized testing in every school in Georgia. When scores are published, schools are ranked by the students' scores and no modifications or exemptions are made for classes with large ESOL populations. As we tell teachers in schools whose rankings are low, remember that the children who may be scoring the lowest need their teachers the most! Yes, it is hard for some teachers to maintain their morale working against the difficulties presented by standardized testing and by working with large populations of ESOL students. On the other hand, many ESOL specialist teachers tell us that they would not trade their jobs for any other, because their students are trying so hard to learn and are so appreciative.

QUESTIONS/REFLECTIONS

1. Get a school report card or look on the Internet for demographic information about a school where you will have a field experience. What are the percentages of white students, African American students, Asians, Hispanics, and other minorities? Find out the percentages of free- and reduced-lunch recipients as indicators of the socioeconomic levels of the school's population.

2. Are there schools in your areas with significant percentages of non–English-speaking students? Visit those schools and/or complete a field experience in one. What are the challenges of teaching the curriculum to all students when many are language minority?

3. During a field experience, get permission to interview an at-risk student. Ask this child about his/her goals, dreams, and hopes for the future. What would you do if you were this child's teacher to provide hope to the student? How do you provide hope for other at-risk students?

CHAPTER 5

What Teachers Do

Ask 10 different teachers to describe their typical day and you will get 10 very different answers. However, there are generalities to what teachers do. Teachers organize and manage students, curriculum, and the resources they use to teach. They also serve as psychologists, nurses, parents, entertainers, and yes, even babysitters. In today's schools teachers are assuming more and more leadership duties—making decisions on everything from which books to buy to which students to expel from school. Teachers may serve on committees to hire new teachers and will definitely be charged with helping the new teachers to survive and succeed at their jobs. Some teachers serve as union representatives and bargain contracts and working conditions for their school and district's teachers. Almost all teachers have extra-curricular and community-related duties to fulfill. Teaching is a time-consuming job and one that puts its employees in the public eye.

A TYPICAL DAY FOR ELEMENTARY TEACHERS

While elementary teachers will be the first to say that every day is different, their schedules are based on teaching a group of 20 to 30 students for the entire day. Some schools start early, with teachers expected to be at school by 7:30 or so. Most days find teachers starting to work with students by 8 A.M. Some of the first duties of the day are attendance, lunch counts, homework checks, and collection of monies for milk, ice cream, and special events. Many classes start with sharing time, which is also a time to calm students and prepare them for academics. Young children bring their personal traumas to school with them, and teachers find that allowing time for sharing of stories helps students to settle into a routine for the day. Some teachers start the day by having students write in journals as a settling activity. Others post lists of students who are assigned to learning centers around the room to start the day. While students work in small groups at these stations, the teacher is free to deal with individual students who have a crisis or need special attention. Announcements and the pledge of allegiance are still a part of the start of most school days.

Reading and language arts are stressed in most elementary schools and significant time is spent in the teaching of reading at this level. In fact, when asked what they would like to change about their day, many teachers say that they would simply like more uninterrupted time for teaching. Language arts is taught in a variety of ways. While there is still whole-group instruction, where the teacher instructs all students at once, many teachers make use of small groups for the teaching of reading, writing, and other language arts activities. For example, a first-grade teacher may divide the class into five groups, with each group working at clusters of desks. While the teacher works with one group on reading comprehension, another group may be reading books of their choice silently, a third group may be drawing pictures of a book that they read yesterday, and a fourth group may be writing sentences about their book. The fifth group may be taking turns at reading a book into a tape recorder. After a determined amount of time, the groups change to another activity, so that each gets time in the teacher's group.

While reading is definitely stressed in elementary school, so too is mathematics. Math, science, and social studies are covered every day, but may not have a certain amount of time allotted for their study. Subjects are often taught together or are covered in interdisciplinary units. Elementary teachers tend to plan units of study around certain topics, such as transportation, communication, pollution, the earth, and so forth, and then teach all subjects through these units. The books that the children read are related to the current unit being taught, and the science and social studies topics are covered within the unit as well. Math may be integrated or it may be taught alone.

Lunch is usually very short—about half an hour. Teachers may be expected to accompany their students to the cafeteria or may have a duty-free lunch. Art and music may be offered once a week by a specialist teacher, or the classroom teacher may be expected to include art and music in his/her own planning. The same is true of health and physical education. Some schools have specialist teachers who take the students for a prescribed time every day, but some schools delegate this subject back to the classroom teacher as well. Some teachers will have students taken out of their classes for speech therapy, special education, extra reading help, and counseling. The classroom door is sometimes a revolving door, with students and special teachers coming and going throughout the day.

If the school has specialist teachers for art, music, physical education, or foreign language, then the time that the students are with the specialist is the time that the classroom teacher plans lessons for the next day and next week. When do elementary teachers go to the bathroom? Whenever they get the chance! For adults used to working in an office with set break times for coffee, the pace of elementary teaching seems exceptionally hectic. The good news seems to be that school days end between 2:30 and 3:30. Most teachers begin planning, organizing, and gathering materials for the next day after the students have left. This is also the time for grading papers, meeting with parents, and for faculty meetings, although some meetings take place before the school day. Teachers are generally expected to work in their rooms for at least half an hour after students leave, before they can leave for home. Again, most teachers who actually leave when their contracts permit carry a large bag of papers and books home where they will continue their grading and planning.

While some elementary teachers have paraprofessionals who assist or aid them in the classroom, the majority still do not. Paraprofessionals can do many of the day-to-day administrative duties, such as the lunch counts, money collections, and so forth. Some grade papers and teach mini-lessons. Many teachers with paraprofessionals report that they are indeed lifesavers for them, allowing them to concentrate on the teaching of students. Having a second adult in the classroom permits bathroom breaks for the teacher and gives young students another adult role model. Could there be a downside to having a paraprofessional in the classroom? If that adult is not well trained, the teacher may spend more of his/her time working with the paraprofessional, which actually takes away time from children and lesson planning. Some districts only give a paraprofessional to large classes, for example, assigning a paraprofessional to a classroom whenever the enrollment tops 28 or 30 students. Some teachers prefer smaller enrollments without the paraprofessional to larger enrollments with one. As with everything in education, there are pros and cons to the paraprofessional situation.

There will always be evenings throughout the school year when teachers are expected to be back at school. Since most parents work, parent conferences tend to be scheduled during evening hours now. There will be at least one or two open houses to meet parents each year and at least one or two nights of scheduled parent conferences. Parent-teacher associations may meet monthly. Yes, all of the textbooks say that teachers choose this profession so that they can have the hours of work that mirror the hours their own children are in school, but there will always be some evening hours, too.

MIDDLE SCHOOL TEACHERS

Middle schools vary widely in their scheduling, but most middle-grade teachers do not see the same students all day. They may see several classes of 25 to 30 students for one or two subjects during the day. Since teaming, both of students and of teachers, is such a part of the middle school concept, teachers at this level will spend significant time working with their colleagues to plan the units, lessons, and topics that they will cover with their team of students.

In large middle schools, students are often assigned a team of teachers in one hallway, creating a "school within a school" concept. This concept helps students as they make the change from their elementary school to the high school.

Middle school teachers often begin their day by being homeroom teachers. The homeroom teacher is expected to know the students well enough to provide them with extra help and counseling. After all, adolescents in the middle school are experiencing a time of emotional and physical growth. They need tremendous amounts of help with growing up and fitting in during these years.

Middle schools are also places for pre–high school exploratory classes. Many middle school teachers have the opportunity to teach outside their field or to teach a hobby during exploratory classes. It is not uncommon for mini-courses to be offered in chess, foreign language, special computer programming, TV production, or other fields in today's middle schools.

Middle school teachers are also charged with preparing students for high school, both academically and in their advisement. Some middle school teachers will help their students choose college preparatory courses or vocational courses at the end of middle school.

What are the special challenges of middle school teaching? These students change dramatically from one day to the next. Their hormones and their emotional development sometimes make teaching academics a challenge. Middle school teachers must really strive to make coursework relevant and must work hard to keep students involved. Many students get lost in middle school and become at-risk students at this time. Middle school teachers do spend a lot of time as counselors and confidantes of their students.

Students at the middle school level are generally not grouped or tracked by ability level. This can be challenging as the teacher may have students who are reading at the college level in a language arts class with students reading at the second-grade level. Imagine the diversity of their writing levels, also.

The positive side to teaching at the middle grades is the dynamic energy that these students have. When middle school children are excited about their learning, they are *really* excited and this enthusiasm can be very rewarding for their teachers.

HIGH SCHOOL TEACHING

I was a high school teacher for eight years and my typical day included six 50-minute classes to be taught every day. High school teachers generally have five or six classes per day, or they have three 90-minute blocked classes per day. High school teachers always talk about their "preps," which are the number of different preparations they have to make in order to teach their classes. I used to have four preps per day, two sections of Spanish 1, two sections of Spanish 2, one section of Spanish 3, and one of Spanish 4. Sometimes, I tried to write different tests for the two sections of Spanish 1 and 2, because I knew that the students talked over lunch and in their physical education classes, so if I didn't write two tests, the second section knew what questions were on the test.

Blocked scheduling increased in popularity in the 1990s and is still popular in many regions. The advantage of teaching for 80 or 90 minutes at a time is that the teacher has more time for activities and in-depth labs or discussions. Teachers often like seeing fewer students per day, for longer amounts of time, than having a revolving door of students going in and out all day. A complaint from teachers who teach on the block schedule is that they can't hold the students' attention for 90 minutes at a time.

It is very rewarding to see your students excel academically—to read their essays, witness their "A's," and watch their growth. One of the best rewards is attending graduation, knowing that you helped these young people graduate, win scholarships, get accepted into college, or get their first real jobs.

While academics are at the heart of high school teaching, there are still many times when a teacher at this level may feel like the babysitter, or the counselor, parent, or psychologist for these students. Just because 17-year-olds look all grown up, doesn't mean that they are. High school teachers deal with drug abuse, alcoholism, child abuse, and a myriad of other problems in working with their students. Many high school students have children of their own, work 20 to 40 hours a week, and may not live with either parent. Truancy remains a large problem for high schools. High school teachers who believe that most of their work will be stimulating minds and grading papers should really pay attention in educational psychology class and take to heart the fact that teenagers are often not focused on academics. High school teachers have to know how to motivate teenagers and how to help them deal with everything from bulimia to violence, and they also have to prepare them for the real world of work or college. It is a challenge.

High schools generally start around 8 A.M. and end around 3:30, but there are dozens of before- and after-school activities for the students, which must be supervised by the teachers. High schools are very busy places, with sports, band, chorus, clubs, service projects, and social activities seeming to dominate the school calendar. In my own eight years as a high school teacher I supervised the Spanish club, the French club, the student council, the National Honor Society, a homecoming parade, many homecoming floats, over a dozen dances, one prom, three field trips, several fundraisers, and sold hot dogs at home football games. I also took students abroad during four summers. The good news about working with students outside of class is that it really helps you get to know them, and it often helps to motivate them in class.

EXTRA-CURRICULAR DUTIES

Jokes abound that if you really want to be a high school social studies teacher, you better be able to coach at least three sports. Extra-curricular duties usually mean sports, band, chorus, and cheerleading. The duties also include club sponsorships, service learning projects, plays, yearbooks, school newspapers, and social activities. Some extra-curricular duties will involve working with teachers and not students—union committees, curriculum planning, book purchasing, planning student orientations, and teacher social events.

These extra-curricular duties are not just limited to the high school teachers. Middle school teachers are called upon to work with their students in most of the same areas as high school programs. In fact, some high schools put intense pressure on their middle school coaches to ensure that athletes are prepared for sports. In middle schools, it is expected that every child have opportunities to explore interests, so middle school clubs will have large enrollments, as will middle school teams and bands.

Even elementary schools have plays, bands, sports, cheerleaders, clubs, and social activities. At the elementary school, teachers may be expected to serve on many parent/teacher committees for school improvement projects and fundraisers. Participation in these extra duties make teachers an integral part of the community where they work.

Will you be paid extra for your extra duties? Yes, in many districts you will be paid extra, especially for sports and coaching, since these duties are really "in the public eye" and may actually earn money for your school. Many teachers say that they can afford to be teachers because they also coach sports. Other duties sometime receive extra payments, too. Teachers' unions negotiate pay for extra-curricular duties, outlining all payments in the group contract. Many elementary schools now accept students as early as 6:30 A.M. and offer after-school programs as late as 8 P.M. If you are asked to participate in these extended-day offerings, you should definitely be paid for your work.

Beware of signing a contract that says, "and extra duties as assigned." While your participation in events outside of the classroom will enhance your relationships with students, parents, and the community, you need to limit your duties to ones in which you have training and experience. You also need to recognize that the first few years your classroom teaching duties will absorb huge amounts of your time in planning and gathering resources. Don't overdo and burn out before you are barely started in the profession.

COMMUNITY EXPECTATIONS ABOUT YOUR LIFESTYLE

A quick study of the history of education will reveal that teachers were restricted from dancing in public and dating during the school year once upon a time. Old contracts had clauses for dismissing teachers who were not seen at church on a regular basis. Many teachers' contracts had morality clauses, and the local board could decide just exactly what constituted immoral behavior. Expectant mothers, married or not, had to quit their teaching duties as soon as they "began to show." While the times have changed, there remain certain expectations about the teacher's lifestyle in a community.

Teachers are role models. Students really do look up to their teachers and look to them for guidance and support. For some students, the teacher is the only adult with whom they have regular contact that is a college graduate. I vividly remember being asked by a junior in high school what it was like to go to college. No one in his family had attended college, and he was afraid to try to attend. I immediately began counseling him about his college options and was very pleased that he completed two years at a community college before going into the world of work.

As role models, we do have to think about what we do "in the public eye." Newspapers always cover the stories of teachers arrested for DUIs and felonies on the front page, and many states and districts have maintained a code of ethics for their educators. As a high school principal recently told student teachers, "Think about what you do before you do it." He shared a story about two teachers having a pitcher of beer with their pizza at a local restaurant. Students were in the restaurant and saw their teachers leave the restaurant, driving home. How much validity will those teachers have when they teach health classes about not drinking and driving? This principal said, "I know my teachers drink beer. I know that I drink beer. I just have to remember that I can be seen by students, and that I have to have a designated driver when I have beer with my pizza." This story is an excellent example of meeting community expectations as a teacher.

What other expectations will be placed on you as a teacher? The expectations vary widely from community to community in different regions of the country. If you plan to live and teach in a small rural community, the expectations of the community for your behavior may be stricter than if you live in a large city and commute out to a suburban school. In any community there will be expectations for your behavior because you are a public employee and are paid with tax dollars.

TEACHER ACCOUNTABILITY

After all is said and done, you are responsible for student learning in the academic fields. Your students will be tested by you, by the district, the state, and possibly by national tests. Your students' grades and test scores will be compared to those of other students in your building, district, and state. There are national rankings of the 50 states with regard to ACT and SAT scores, and there are international comparisons of students' scores in math, science, and reading. Will your students make the grade? Will you? Should your students' grades and achievement scores on standardized tests determine if you will be rehired? These questions are currently hot topics of debate around the country.

What can you do to ensure the best education for your students? You should definitely know the curriculum that you are supposed to be teaching. Ask in your job interview if the district has written curriculum guides. Who wrote them and are the guides aligned with the textbooks used and the tests administered? It is obvious that if you are not teaching the material that appears on end-of-the-year tests, your students will not do as well. The alignment of what is taught and what is tested is critical in achieving high test scores. However, teachers also need to be careful of not simply "teaching to the test." There must be a variety of teaching methods and a variety of assessment methods used to ensure your students' achievement.

Are you responsible for your students' safety and well-being while they are at school? Let's look at that question from another point of view. If you are the parent of a student, do you feel that your child's teacher is accountable for both academic learning and your child's safety? This question has become increasingly more difficult for teachers. While we all expect teachers to do everything within their power to teach and protect students, it is also recognized that teachers alone cannot guarantee the safety of their students at all times. Again, news stories report that school violence and school safety are major issues with the American public. What *can* you do? Always understand your school's policies and follow procedures for violence prevention. Make sure that you have backup support by knowing who to call in case of an emergency in your classroom. Take student threats seriously and be aware of cliques and loners in your classes. Above all, attend the training that your school offers about conflict resolution and violence prevention before the school year starts.

QUESTIONS/REFLECTIONS

1. As a field experience, arrange to shadow a teacher throughout an entire school day. Begin the day when he/she does and do not leave the school until he/she does. Record the amount of time spent with students and the amount of time spent in extra-curricular duties.

2. Interview a teacher who teaches the grade and/or subject that you intend to teach. Ask them how many hours per week they really work. Their total should include all activities and the work that they do at home grading papers and planning lessons. How does this number of hours compare to a 40-hour workweek?

3. Ask practicing teachers about the community expectations of their behavior. Were these expectations actually stated to them when they accepted their jobs or did they just hear about the expectations informally? Do they know of any faculty members who lost their jobs because of their public behaviors?

CHAPTER 6

The Purpose of Schools, Their Role in the Community, and How They Are Run

Think back to your years in elementary, middle, and high school. Was your school an integral part of the community? Were plays, concerts, and sports events well attended? Did any businesspeople or community leaders attend your classes and share experiences or mentor students? Did anyone make donations to your schools—computers, uniforms, or school supplies? How much influence did the federal and state governments have on the curriculum and day-to-day school business? Was your school the best in the state? How did its scores rate against national and international standards?

What did you know about the people who ran the school—the school board members, the superintendent, the principal, and other administrators? Can you name your principals, the superintendents, and any board members? Were their pictures in the local newspaper? Did they seem to be respected and well liked? Were there complaints about them and how they ran the school? Were there ever any scandals about school leaders?

What did you know about the actual working conditions of the teachers? Did the teachers have a union? What did your teachers say about how the schools were run? Were their comments positive or negative? Did you know their salaries? Did they complain about their salaries?

Think about these questions as you read about the link between schools and communities. How much influence does a community have on its schools and how much can the school change the community?

A VERY SHORT HISTORY OF THE PURPOSE OF SCHOOLS

To fully understand the school's role in the community, we have to consider the purposes of schools in general. If the school's purpose is to educate children and young people, then what does it mean to be educated? Historically, schools were founded in this country so that males could know the Bible, and so that they would have the skills to earn a living and to govern society. Some would argue that the need for education to create a literate citizenry still exists and that only a knowledgeable population can self-govern. For many years education was denied to segments of the population so that they would remain voiceless and powerless.

As the nation grew and became industrialized, many felt that the purpose of the schools was to produce good workers. Good workers would be able to read, write, do arithmetic, and have a strong work ethic. Good workers can build a strong economy and a strong country.

Others view the purpose of schools not from the point of view of creating citizens and workers, but of developing human potential. They believe that the best education allows students to "find themselves" and their destinies by studying until they discover their own potential. The search for identity will create happy individuals who understand life.

Still others believe that schools should remain true institutions of pure learning, where all students master the classics, learn philosophy, mathematics, and all the subjects that will give them a true liberal arts and sciences education. Knowing the classics will make these students truly "educated."

As our society has grown, it has developed its own social ills, and some now believe that it is the purpose of the schools to be "the great equalizer." People who see the schools in this light believe that an education can jump-start a student out of poverty and into the middle or upper class. Our society is now looking to the schools to educate students about drugs, alcohol, sex, violence, and all the challenges of living in the modern world.

There are indeed many purposes for our schools—including being the parent, babysitter, and social world for today's youth. With all of the purposes for schools, it is not a surprise that the federal, state, and local governments all play a part in the governance and mission of schools in every community.

THE SCHOOL'S ROLE IN THE COMMUNITY

So just what is the school's role in the community? Is the school responsible for creating good citizens, efficient workers, happy individuals, clear-thinking scholars, and saving the world from the evils that exist? This is quite a challenge, indeed. As a teacher, it is hoped that you think about these global issues past your history and foundations of education course. The truth is that you will see the school where you work in a more practical, down-to-earth light. In a small town or large city, the schools will constantly be in the news. When new residents move into a community, realtors sell them homes by boasting about the schools. In fact, realtors may be the first people to demand the updated school report cards about which neighborhood schools have excelled at standardized tests. All schools now publish data about their achievement tests, graduation rates, and college entrance percentages, so communities know where their schools stand. If the school's scores are low, some vocal community members may be addressing the board and school leaders for reform and change.

Schools remain social centers for their communities, offering sports events, plays, concerts, and student showcases of work. Many schools are becoming more all-inclusive, offering health and family-related services to the children and their families that were once only offered by social service agencies. Daycare centers in public schools are more and more common, with some schools accommodating children from 7 A.M. to 7 or 8 P.M. Many schools will open their facilities for public use as a polling place during elections, as a site for Boy Scout or Girl Scout functions, for community meetings, and other functions. After all, who owns the schools? The communities own the schools, public tax dollars pay for the schools, and elected community members govern the schools.

WHO IS YOUR BOSS?

If the community owns the school, is the community your boss? If the taxpayers pay your salary, are they your boss? Are the students your boss? In some ways, the answer to each of these questions is "yes." On the practical side, the community elects its representatives to the local school board, the board then hires a superintendent and building principals, who serve as your boss. Many teachers get to know their board members well because they visit schools and individual classes regularly. Other times, a teacher may never actually meet or know a board member personally, although you should know who they are.

The superintendent is really the chief executive officer of the school district, and as a CEO he/she may or may not get to know individual teachers closely. Your principal should get to know you well, since he/she will probably evaluate you for reemployment. However, in some schools, even the building principal does not interact with teachers on a daily basis, and an assistant principal or curriculum director evaluates teachers' performance for renewed employment.

Once you are hired, you will know who your immediate boss is, and he/she should clearly explain the expectations of your job to you before the school year begins. As a public school teacher, you will always serve multiple constituencies, including the students, their parents, the taxpayers, the community, and yes, even the general public. If you choose to work at a private school, the governance and management of that school will be determined by the constituents who have founded (and funded) the school. Some private schools are governed by the churches that run them, and others are designed by the directors who have built the school. There are certainly private schools that exist to make money, and those schools may indeed be run in a very similar manner to businesses. Public or private, the administration of the school where you work will expect a well-trained, caring professional to teach the students in the classroom.

As a teacher, you will know much more about the principal, superintendent, and board members than you did as a student in school. You should guard what you say about your bosses to your students, because students take what you say very seriously, and they repeat what you say publicly. Teachers not only teach their students, but they have a huge role in public relations between the school and the community. The best advice you can receive is to always act professionally in all of your communications. There may be times when the local newspaper or TV station carries a story or scandal about the school administration or board members and your responses to student questions can go a long way in curbing more negative attention to the situation.

As you work, you may want to observe your bosses because you may want to become a principal or superintendent someday. There is a need for good administrators and there is a shortage in some parts of the country. If management and school leadership interest you, you can pursue an advanced degree and certification to become one of the "bosses."

LINKS BETWEEN SCHOOLS AND BUSINESS

In the 1980s, schools began receiving televisions and VCRs from companies that made this equipment available in exchange for a guarantee that the students would watch a certain number of minutes of television programming. The programming consisted of news and human interest stories designed for young people, and, of course, there were commercials. Most schools jumped on the bandwagon for the free equipment. It can be argued that this is a good example of big business helping schools, and it can be argued that this is an example of big business taking advantage of schools by using them to solicit new customers. Both sides of the argument have their points.

Schools and businesses can be linked in many ways. Businesses may already be paying significant taxes in support of the local schools where they are located. Business leaders may choose to run for the school board and serve as leaders in that capacity. Businesses are frequently asked to make donations to schools for additional supplies, special trips, yearbooks, and computers. With donations may come heightened interest in school programs, and with heightened interest there may come "strings." The strings attached may be formal or informal pressure to make the changes that the business leaders seek. Some of these changes may be very good ones that the school might not have implemented without the pressure from the business world.

High schools continue to have strong ties to businesses through school-to-work programs and internships for seniors. Mentoring has received much positive attention lately, and mentoring programs exist to help high school students decide on career choices. Mentors can serve as adult role models to students of all ages in schools. As your teaching career continues, you will probably see more and more partnerships with businesses, as schools take on the idea that "it takes a village to raise a child."

PARENTS AND OTHER PARTNERS

Parents are the child's first and most enduring teachers. Therefore, the school's outreach and partnerships with parents are extremely important. Parents should be welcomed to the school at the beginning of every school year, and there should be several open houses and opportunities for teachers to meet with parents. Parents should know when and how to contact their child's teacher, and the teacher should make every effort to contact parents early in the year with a positive note, phone call, or newsletter.

As a teacher, you will quickly realize that not all of your students live with both parents, or even one parent. Start thinking of parents, guardians, and other caregivers in the role of the traditional parent. Word your letters accordingly, so that letters home are addressed to the parents, guardians, or caregivers of your students. If you are a parent or caregiver, always think about treating your students' caregivers the way that you would want your own child's teacher to treat you. I first heard this in a workshop, and I think it is the best advice I can imagine for teachers who are parents and for those who aren't.

What can parents do to be involved in their child's education? First and foremost, it is hoped that the parents/guardians send their child to school ready to learn. This means that the parent should make sure the child gets enough sleep, a balanced diet, and the appropriate clothing and other basic needs. As simple as this sounds, it often doesn't happen. As a teacher, you can't doubly punish students whose parents have already punished them by not caring for them. Remember, a teacher accepts all students as they are and then helps each to succeed. If you can't accept children who come to school dirty, hungry, and in need of attention, teaching is the not the field for you. You can, however, be an advocate for these children and work to get school support to help them. Psychologists tell us that optimal learning doesn't take place until basic needs are met.

Parents can be very helpful volunteers in the schools. Some schools have parent volunteers who answer the phones in the school office every morning, who take attendance, lunch counts, milk money, and make sure that the day is off to a good start before they return home. Other parents come to the school in the afternoon and serve as bus monitors, making sure students get on the right bus home. When parents take care of these duties, the teachers are freed to work with students who need academic help or to make lesson plans.

Some parents make excellent classroom volunteers, serving as listeners when young students read, copying papers at the photocopy machine, or serving as an aide to the teacher. Many parents who can't give of their time during the school day can volunteer to bring in snacks or to work on fundraisers that take place after school or on weekends. At the middle and high school levels, parents can attend events to show their

support, chaperone band and sports events, volunteer to clean uniforms, and also provide snacks for extra-curricular events. They can be
tremendous fundraisers and sometimes the high school bands and cho-
ruses just wouldn't exist without the efforts of the parent booster clubs.

In order to make parent volunteer efforts work, someone at the
school must organize the parents and train them with regard to their
roles and responsibilities. Having parents show up at the classroom
door with cookies or cupcakes at an inopportune time may indeed
thwart a third-grade teacher's math lesson. Having parents in your
room will hopefully show them the demands of your job and how good
you are at it. Having parents in your room will also mean that you better be organized and ready and really be teaching! Your accountability
may be on the line when visitors come in frequently. Parents can actually cause some disruptions and might also want to tell you what and
how to teach. So, while you are busy building bridges to make parents
your partners in education, remember that there may be times when you
need to close the classroom door and just teach, using parent volunteers
in another way.

If, as the old saying goes, it does take a village to raise a child, then
there are other partners in addition to businesses and parents to be considered. Some look to the police officers in the community as partners
in education. The police officers can talk to students about the dangers
of alcohol, drugs, and violence, and many schools have an officer assigned to them by the police department for public relations. Sometimes students who are convicted of felonies are assigned to school in
lieu of jail, and the teachers and probation officers must work closely
together to ensure that those students are meeting the requirements of
their sentences.

The child welfare agencies in each state and community can play an
integral role in helping schools. These agencies can help children who
show signs of neglect and abuse, and when the school has a good working relationship with its child welfare agency, the steps for getting help
for a student will be easier. Hopefully, the child welfare agency is also
offering training to parents who need help dealing with their stresses
and those of their children.

Teachers today do not have the luxury of teaching pure academics in
a vacuum. An earlier chapter mentioned that the classroom door is often a revolving door because of special teachers who enter and leave
and because of the special pull-out programs for children. The classroom door is also an open door to parents, businesses, and community

service organizations. The door is open because teaching is a public service and viewed as a public activity. You, as a teacher, are also considered a caregiver in your students' lives. Don't try to do everything by yourself, but reach out to the partners who can help you to deal with the students so that you can get back to the business of teaching.

SCHOOL AS A WORKPLACE

I worked every summer that I was in college. One summer my job was at a 4-H camp, another year my job was at a hotel, and the last two years of college I actually worked in a factory. Each of those workplaces was unique, and it can be argued that the school as a workplace is quite different from the business world. Do teachers punch a time clock as I did in my factory job? Yes, at some schools they do. At other schools, teachers sign in at the main office and sign out at the end of the day. Some schools do not require signing in or punching the time clock—teachers are just expected to be on site 30 minutes before and after the student school day. I know one principal who stays at school until every teacher has signed out for the day. Around 5:30 P.M., he makes an announcement on the intercom that it really is time to go home and asks all remaining teachers to say goodbye for the day. (He feels that teachers should not work in the school at night, due to crime and safety concerns.)

Many teachers feel that their jobs do give them much independence and freedom with regard to decision making. As author Carol Fuery (1990, p. 5) wrote about her classroom:

> I consider myself a small business owner. I rent office space, my classroom, from the principal. Sure, I still have a curriculum guide to follow, but I'm an independent operator. When my classroom door closes, I have a lot of freedom. As the teacher, I'm the CEO, the chief executive officer.

Other teachers may argue that they could run the school better without the mandates, rules, and constraints constantly placed upon them by the administration. They feel that they have lost much of their freedom to do what they know is best for students because of standardized tests, watered-down curriculum, and the accountability movement. Some teachers report that they simply cannot achieve success because of the students' social problems and lack of parental support.

Many teachers feel that they are not treated as professionals in the workplace. They don't have office space or telephones at their disposal. Often, teachers must still go to the main office to make or receive a telephone call, knowing that the office secretary will hear the conversation. (Of course many teachers bring their cell phones to work; at some schools, however, this is not permitted.) Some schools are very overcrowded, forcing teachers to share classrooms throughout the day. Older buildings lack air conditioning and are simply not kept clean. I know many teachers who still sweep and dust their own classrooms because they refuse to work in a dirty environment. Are computer programmers, stock brokers, lawyers, and engineers forced to sweep their offices? I doubt it. Is it difficult to demand a cleaner work environment? Yes, it is, especially when one is a new or nontenured teacher. When asked why I left high school teaching for college teaching, I have even been known to say, "I just couldn't stand the thought of working in a hot, dirty classroom where I didn't have the space I needed to be the best teacher I could be."

However, many schools have improved greatly and their physical facilities provide a much better work environment than some businesses. There are schools that provide clean classrooms and work spaces for their teachers. Some teachers have phones on their desks, as well as state-of-the-art computers in their rooms. Many teachers carry business cards, and their schools pay for professional workshops and conferences. When you interview for your first position, ask to tour the school and to see the classroom where you would work. Ask about opportunities for continued education and conferences.

The teacher is always in a "front-line" position. If you are absent, the school must find a substitute for you. This type of responsibility is demanding and creates a workplace with high demands and stressors. You can't take a coffee break whenever you want because you simply cannot leave your students unsupervised. You can't just talk on the phone or send e-mails from your desk to conduct your personal business during the day when you are a teacher. You are onstage and active all the time. Teaching is fast-paced and hectic, but the excitement of working with students is very rewarding. In teaching I get to problem solve constantly, rather than just pull covers for books on the assembly line of the factory where I worked those summers. By the nature of the job, teaching is different from the business world, with both advantages and disadvantages. Good advice to someone considering teaching would be to get as much experience as possible in both worlds before deciding on your career.

QUESTIONS/REFLECTIONS

1. While visiting a school for your field experience, be sure to find the teachers' workroom, restrooms, and lounge areas. Are they clean and well maintained? Are phones and computers available? What do teachers say about the support they receive from custodians and maintenance staff?

2. What is the purpose of the school? Are teachers just babysitters sometimes? Ask a teacher to describe his/her opinion about the role of the school in creating citizens, workers, or well-rounded individuals.

3. How can teachers work to improve the school as a workplace? Can unions play a role in the school's environment?

CHAPTER 7

The Professional Life of the Teacher

Noted educator Harry K. Wong has said that there are four stages in the professional life of a teacher—fantasy, survival, mastery, and impact (1998, p. 5, 291). Fantasy is where the newly hired teacher believes that everything is wonderful and that all students are learning the material presented. Fantasy may be called the honeymoon by some and may only last a few weeks. Survival is where the beginning teacher exhibits behaviors that help him/her to make it to the end of the week, the semester, and the school year. Ironically, I have seen some veteran teachers remain at the survival stage. The mastery stage includes teachers who have gone beyond survival and who practice wonderful teaching strategies that enhance authentic student learning. Most principals call teachers in this stage their "master" teachers—and it has nothing to do with having a master's degree. The highest stage in Wong's model is called impact, because teachers at this stage "make an impact not only on the lives of their students, but also on their own lives and the life of the community" (p. 291). A young teacher or a veteran can teach at the impact level, depending on attitude, experience, training, and commitment on the part of the teacher, and the support received from school administration and community.

THE LIFE CYCLE OF THE TEACHER

Referred to as "career stages" by Steffy (1989), and categorized into life cycle stages by Steffy et al. (2000), your teaching career will definitely have its own ups, downs, periods of burnout, and times of renewal. Go back to the list of teachers that you made in the introduction to this book.

Were any of your teachers "brand new" to the teaching profession when they were your teachers? Were these teachers just 22 years old or were they new to teaching after having worked in another profession? Did you have a lot of young teachers when you were a student? If so, what did these teachers do differently than the older, veteran teachers? Some may argue that new teachers lack experience, but others say that a new teacher's energy and enthusiasm make up for any shortcomings. Principals agree that a new teacher's zest for teaching and a belief that all children can learn make new teachers real assets to the teaching faculty.

Let's go through your list and identify those teachers who had at least 8 to 10 years of experience. Had those teachers developed into true "master" teachers? Did they help all children to learn? Were they organized and "with-it"? Did you look forward to going to their classes?

Did you have any teachers who were near to and counting the years and/or days until their retirement? Were these teachers still inspiring you and the other students? Did you have any teachers who didn't finish the school year because of burnout, stress, or illness? How old was that teacher and how long had he/she been teaching? While burnout is real, some veteran teachers offer a wealth of experience to their students and to their colleagues. When I was a beginning teacher, I had the privilege of teaching near a veteran history teacher who was also a World War II navy veteran. When he taught about the war, his stories made his classroom come alive. Both students and teachers were awed by this man who had lived the history that he taught.

Because people enter the field of teaching from many different tracks today—traditional undergraduate programs, post-baccalaureate teacher certification, graduate programs—there is no one "career plan" for all teachers. Some teachers may still enter the profession at age 22 and teach for 40 years. Other individuals may not decide on teaching until they reach their 40s, 50s, or 60s, and are searching for a complete change in their lives. I once heard a motivational speaker who said that the average career of a classroom teacher in the midwest was 13 years. If this is true, then some teachers are indeed leaving early and others are entering the profession late.

THE EARLY YEARS OF TEACHING

No matter how one enters the teaching profession, the first year of teaching will be memorable. The first year has moments of euphoria and points of extreme frustration. Some first-year teachers do not complete their first year because of the challenges they face. It has been said that first-year teachers get the worst classes, the most difficult assignments, and the leftover classrooms and resources. The term "reality shock" is used to describe the feelings that beginning teachers have about coming face-to-face with the real world of teaching. "Reality shock begins as apprentice teachers, working alone, assume total responsibility and accountability for the planning, classroom management, instruction, and student assessment" (Clement, Enz, & Pawlas, 2000, p. 45).

Teaching is different from other professions because new teachers are expected to assume all the duties of veteran teachers from the first moment of the first day of the new school year. The experience gained in student teaching helps immeasurably, but even in student teaching the cooperating teacher was always there to answer questions, preapprove lesson plans, and serve as a safety net for the novice. Are there safety nets for first-year teachers?

More and more school districts have implemented induction programs that support beginning teachers. A good induction program can include orientation at the beginning of the school year, a series of seminars throughout the school year, and an assigned mentor for the new teacher. Orientation workshops that are held before the students arrive will help the new teacher to learn the specific rules and guidelines of the district. Orientation workshops can include time for the new teacher to work in the classroom and prepare the bulletin boards, seating charts, and plans for the first day. Since new teachers will be quite overwhelmed at the beginning of the year, later seminars designed just for new teachers can be very worthwhile if they are offered throughout the school year. The content of the seminars should be timed to coincide with the flow of the school year. For example, offering a half-day seminar about how to communicate with parents a week before the first parent open house is timely. Support seminars that help new teachers deal with classroom management, grading, student motivation, special education, and their own stress management will be particularly helpful as the school year progresses. While all teachers need a venue for discussing their concerns, problems, and successes, it is especially important that new teachers have the opportunities to do so in a safe environment. This type of staff development should be provided during the school day, not at the end of a trying, tiring day when all the teacher really wants to do is to simply go home.

Mentoring continues to increase in popularity in both the business and education worlds. Mentoring programs vary in goals and scope, but all strive to increase the success of the new employee. In teaching, the mentor serves as a role model to the new teacher, and may also serve as a confidante, nonevaluative observer, guide, and friend. Some mentors are volunteers who teach across the school hall and see their role as simply answering questions for new teachers. Other mentors are in a more formalized role, working closely with new teachers throughout the year, attending seminars and workshops together. Some mentors are paid to work with new teachers as an "extra duty" in lieu of coaching a sport or sponsoring a school-related activity. Other mentors may be released from classroom teaching duties to mentor a number of new teachers full time. Many curriculum directors mentor new teachers through planned observations and peer-coaching activities. A few districts hire recently retired teachers to return as mentors (Clement, Enz, & Pawlas, 2000, p. 55).

On a day-to-day basis a mentor can help a new teacher to find books and supplies, share workable ideas for instruction and classroom management, and listen to new ideas. Mentors share both the formal and informal culture of the school, helping new teachers to "learn the ropes" of their jobs. When searching for your first job, be sure to ask about the kinds of support that will be offered to you during your initial years in the district. A position with a lower salary, but with a trained mentor and some release days for seminars and conferences, may prove to be a better position than a higher-paying position.

STAYING CURRENT AND GROWING PROFESSIONALLY BY JOINING ORGANIZATIONS

Once you have "survived" your first years in teaching, it is time to assess how you will grow professionally. For many teachers, professional growth is equated with staying current. Organizations abound in teaching, and you will need to find one that helps you stay updated in your specific fields, as well as teaching in general.

Many elementary teachers join the International Reading Association (IRA), because it helps them with one of their most primary duties—the teaching of reading. They also may join the Association for Childhood Education International (ACEI) or the National Association for the Education of Young Children (NAEYC). Middle school teachers join the National Middle School Association, as well as organizations that are specific to their fields. High school teachers tend to join the subject-matter specific organizations, such as the National Council of Teachers of English (NCTE), the National Science Teachers Association (NSTA), the National Council for the Teaching of Mathematics (NCTM), the National Council for the Social Studies (NCSS), or one of the associations for foreign languages. There are, of course, associations for each of the special fields of teaching. Health and physical education teachers join the American Alliance for Health, Physical Education, Recreation, and Dance (AAHPERD). Teachers who specialize in students with exceptionalities join the Council for Exceptional Children (CEC) and the National Association for Gifted Children (NAGC). Speech teachers, teachers of bilingual classrooms and teachers of ESOL each have their own organization. They are the Speech Communication Association (SCA), the National Association for Bilingual Education (NABE), and Teachers of English to Speakers of Other Languages (TESOL). Business teachers can join the National Business Education Association (NBEA) and music teachers can join the Music Teachers National Association (MTNA). Many of these associations can be found online at their Websites. For more information, please see the Teacher's Resource Guide in Parkay and Hardcastle Stanford's *Becoming a Teacher* (1998).

How does joining a professional association keep you current? First of all, professional organizations publish newsletters and journals. Reading the publications from your association will help you to find out what other teachers in your field are doing. Anytime you read an article, ask yourself if the new strategy or idea you just read about will work in your classroom. Why or why not? Should you implement the new idea? You will often read about educational reforms in the professional journals and how your field is following the national or international trends. As you read, you may find yourself saying, "I've not only done that, but I've made it work even better than the author." When you start saying this, it is time for you to begin writing articles. Being a professional means having something to profess, and writing your ideas will help to increase the knowledge base of the teaching profession.

In addition to just reading the publications of the association, you can attend local, state, and national conferences. Conferences are a fun way to network with other teachers, get new ideas, and share your joys and concerns. Sometimes it is easier to open up to a teacher from another state than to talk to the teacher in the classroom down the hall.

Again, after you have attended several conferences, share what works in your classroom with other teachers by presenting at a conference.

Becoming a member in one or more of the associations for your subject and grade is just one part of the process of staying current about teaching. The second part is staying informed about the whole field of teaching. As a new teacher you will be asked to join a teachers' association/union in your district. As an experienced teacher, you will most likely be asked to assume a larger role in that association. The NEA and AFT are the two national unions in the United States. Each union has state chapters, as well as local chapters in school districts. Teachers in the district vote to decide which union they want to join. In some states, there exists a third option, that of a state association with local chapters.

What do the NEA and AFT offer? They offer support to teachers for collective bargaining of annual contracts. If your district is at an impasse in negotiating a contract with its board of education, the union has trained professionals to help your local complete negotiations in a timely manner. Yes, they will also help your local to strike if needed. They offer liability insurance to their members as part of a benefit package, and liability insurance is an extremely important asset to a teacher, just as malpractice insurance is a necessity for a medical doctor. Other benefit package opportunities include group travel, insurance, and credit cards. They offer journals and magazines to update teachers about the profession, just as the subject-specific organizations. The unions have national, regional, and state conferences, where they train teachers in how to bargain contracts and work for improved working conditions. At these conferences, staff development is also offered in leadership training, stress management, money management, legal issues, and retirement planning.

The unions are very helpful in supporting teachers to have better workplaces and improved benefits. The unions speak as a lobby to state and national politicians, thereby promoting the concerns of all teachers to the public. Many veteran teachers find working with the union at the local or state level to be very rewarding. After becoming established as teachers, many veterans feel that they want to improve the profession by improving the working conditions for all teachers, and assuming a leadership role in the union is a good way to do so.

Honor societies in education are also valuable to teachers for networking and resources. You may be invited to join an educational honor society while in your undergraduate or graduate teacher education program. Three national educational honor societies are Kappa

Delta Pi, Phi Delta Kappa, and Pi Lambda Theta. Each has publications and national conferences. In this electronic age, it is possible to take advantage of chat rooms offered by these associations for on-line networking with colleagues.

How much will it cost you to join the union, an association for your grade and subject, and an honor society? The total amount of money that you spend on associations and publications will be at least several hundred dollars annually. This is a lot of money, but one has to keep current in the field. Would you like to go to a doctor who hasn't read anything about medicine in the past decade? The field of education is changing and being a professional teacher means that you have to continue learning. Your participation in professional organizations is one vehicle for your continued education.

WHEN AND HOW DO I GO BACK TO SCHOOL?

A commonly asked question by students just receiving their teacher certification is, "When should I get my master's degree?" Thoughtful students ask, "What is the best way to earn my master's and should it be in a subject field or education in general?" Again, as a reminder, all universities vary in how they offer teacher certification, and some students will earn their initial certification with a master's degree. For those who earn their certification with a bachelor's degree, the question of how and when to pursue the master's is a very valid question.

Rumors abound that some districts only want to hire new teachers with a bachelor's degree because they can pay them less than a new teacher with a master's degree. So, some people advise new teachers to get a job first, and then start on their master's after they get tenure in the district. Some professors of education advise recent graduates to get two to three years of experience teaching before starting to earn the master's degree, so that they can balance the theories they will study in the master's program with personal experience.

When a student asks me about the best time to get the master's degree, I always say, "Get your master's degree when YOU have the opportunity to do so." For some students who are accustomed to living in a dorm and not yet having an income, the best time to continue their studies is immediately after their bachelor's degree. Some beginning teachers are also getting married and starting families, and that may not be a good time to go back to college. However, some women get their master's degree while staying home with small children when they are not teaching for a few years. It is very difficult to get a master's while teaching full time, managing a home, new marriage, and a first baby. Do not try to do everything at once.

Why should you get a master's degree at all? First and foremost, the master's will raise your salary, perhaps $4,000 a year or more, and your salary is then elevated throughout your entire teaching career. The higher your salary, the higher your retirement benefits will be as well. Earning a master's degree will enable you to fully understand the theories and research behind what you do on a day-to-day basis. Some districts may require you to get your master's to stay employed. States continue to look at ways to improve the quality of teachers and may require you to get the master's degree. Many states already require teachers to take a certain number of staff development classes to maintain their certification, so you might as well take classes in a planned sequence that lead to a degree, rather than just a hodge-podge of classes with no direction.

Should your master's be in a subject field or in education in general? Many colleges offer a master's degree in elementary education, middle school education, or secondary education. These programs offer a degree that includes courses about specific teaching strategies, such as advanced methods of teaching language arts, as well as courses in the theory of education. Some master's programs in secondary education offer the opportunity to take advanced courses in the subject, such as math, physics, or Spanish literature while also offering courses in the advanced study of curriculum, methods, and the history and philosophy of education.

Other master's programs are designed for teachers who want to become curriculum directors, principals, or superintendents. These programs may be titled as educational administration or educational leadership. Some lead directly to a new certification to be a principal or superintendent, while others give just the master's degree and then the student must take tests or additional coursework from the state for the certification.

Teachers who get their master's in a subject field or in education probably plan to remain classroom teachers. Teachers who are interested in other positions will study educational administration or leadership.

CONTINUING EDUCATION PAST THE MASTER'S DEGREE

After the master's degree, one can pursue an education specialist (Ed.S.) degree, or a doctorate. Again, the Ed.S. adds another jump to the classroom teacher's annual salary. Many principals and superintendents have the education specialist's degree, and have concentrated their studies in administration, leadership, or staff development. Some Ed.S. programs are ones designed specifically for the training of principals and superintendents. Just as a master's degree is generally 32 hours of coursework past the bachelor's degree, the specialist's degree is generally 32 hours past the master's. In addition to coursework, most master's programs have an added requirement of a thesis, project, or of extensive exams. Most specialist programs also have the thesis, project, portfolio, or exam requirement.

If a teacher earns a specialist degree, should he or she consider a doctorate? A specialist degree does not automatically count toward a doctorate. In fact, it is rare if more than half of the courses of the specialist would count toward a doctorate, because doctoral programs emphasize pure research. Pursue a doctorate if you consider teaching at the college level, since even community colleges may require the doctorate. Many principals and superintendents now earn doctoral degrees. Some practicing classroom teachers earn doctorates and remain in their classrooms. They often work with student teachers from nearby colleges and are in high demand upon retirement to work part-time for the university as student teaching supervisors.

The term "life-long learner" is certainly true for the professional teacher. Teachers go to school to teach and then return to college to learn. If you like being a student, teaching is an excellent career choice for you!

NATIONAL BOARD FOR PROFESSIONAL TEACHING STANDARDS

Established in 1987, the National Board for Professional Teaching Standards (NBPTS) offers certificates to practicing teachers with experience who exhibit the highest standards in their classroom teaching. The process for earning NBPTS certification is extremely rigorous, including a portfolio and assessment from a committee. The cost of application was over $2,000 in 2001. Earning this certification does not replace state certification. In fact, those who seek national board certification are already certified teachers with experience. Each state decides how to reward those who earn this prestigious recognition. The process is a reflective one that encourages teachers to study their own teaching practices in order to improve. The national board certification process exists to improve the quality of teaching and to provide recognition to those who are truly master teachers. It is another way for practicing teachers to continue learning. For more information about NBPTS, see their Website at www.nbpts.org.

QUESTIONS/REFLECTIONS

1. Ask six veteran teachers who have their master's degrees to explain how and when they were able to complete that degree. Find a teacher who has an Ed.S. or a doctorate and ask them about the programs that they completed. Would they recommend their program for other teachers?

2. Ask practicing teachers about their district's affiliation with the NEA or the AFT. Do they feel that their union helps them? If so, how? How involved are these teachers in their unions?

3. Go to the Internet and look up two of the professional organizations in your field or the educational honor societies. What are the costs and benefits? Ask practicing teachers which organizations they find useful.

CHAPTER 8

Your Job Search

The decision to become a teacher is indeed a challenging one. Once you have made the decision and have chosen your course of study leading to certification, you will probably ask, "Will I get a job?" For some people, the job offer will come before they receive certification, and those people will be asking, "Should I take this job?" The answers to both questions are the same, "It all depends on you."

Jobs do not just happen. New graduates must make them happen. In the field of teaching, many stories still abound about people who are told by principals from the school districts where they were students that all they have to do is finish a program and a job is waiting for them. In areas with extreme teaching shortages, some superintendents have been known to tell friends to "just go pick up a course or two in education and then we can hire you." Be wary of job offers such as these! The truth is that for you to get a job, there must actually be an opening that is approved by the board of education, and to maintain their accreditation and reputation, districts must hire certified teachers or at least ones who are provisionally certified and completing work toward certification. So, how do you get a job in this profession?

WHERE TO TURN FOR HELP

Your college or university is the first place to turn for help in your job search. The career center (sometimes called the placement office) will publish job openings in school districts, sponsor recruitment fairs that bring personnel directors from school districts to your campus, and help you prepare cover letters and résumés that are appropriate for the field of teaching. Some career centers still maintain placement files for education majors. These files contain letters of recommendation for you, and when you apply for a job, the career center sends a copy of your file to the prospective employer. Placement files are very helpful because you only have to get one letter written from each of your references, yet those letters may then be sent to an infinite number of potential employers by the career center.

The career centers exist on college campuses to help students and alumni find jobs. These offices have current information about teacher shortages, out-of-state and foreign teaching positions, and job fairs held around the state. Some centers now keep student résumés and cover letters in on-line databases and can match a school district's openings directly to you and your résumé. However, the career center can't help you unless you go the office and complete the necessary paperwork—and complete it on time. Most students who use their college's career center find that their job search anxiety is greatly reduced—and that they get jobs!

The Internet has truly revolutionized job searching in most fields, including education. Most state Departments of Education have Websites and many of these Websites also have sections for school districts to post their current job openings. Use the listings found at the back of this book to look at state Department of Education Websites, or just do a search on the Internet for your state. Again, your college career center will have additional Website information available.

ORGANIZING YOUR SEARCH AND YOUR PAPERWORK

You need to decide where you want to teach, considering, of course, where the jobs are. Once you have an idea of where you want to be, go to the career center or start reading on-line for positions that are open where you want to work. You may want to talk to teachers in the schools about possible openings at their schools, remembering that a rumor of a job opening is not the same as a true job opening, and that public schools must follow strict guidelines about advertising and hiring new teachers.

If you are willing to relocate, your chances of getting a job are always much higher. If the job is in another state, however, you will have to get that state's certification, and the rules are different for all states of the United States with regard to teacher certification. Your interest and experience with coaching and student activities will also make you more marketable. Speaking a foreign language or having an endorsement to teach English as a second language may add to your job prospects. If there are teacher shortages in the geographic areas where you are searching for a job, you may be asked to teach outside of your field of certification during the early years of your career. These are all considerations for you to think about as you organize your search and create your paperwork.

Even in times of teacher shortages, some schools have such good reputations that a hundred candidates may apply for the same position. If that is the case, your paperwork, experience, and background will have to be outstanding just to get an interview.

Just what should your job search paperwork include? First and foremost, you must have a résumé. A résumé for a teaching position is different from one for the business world. Your résumé should summarize your educational background, indicating that your training is indeed appropriate for teaching. If you have not completed a teacher certification program, then your education would indicate your background in the subject areas you plan to teach. For example, a bachelor's degree in chemistry for a high school science position indicates your knowledge of what you will teach.

Your work experience should include the field experiences and student teaching completed during your college program. Always include the grades and subjects taught during field experience, as well as the schools, since prospective employers want to know that you have worked with a diverse group of students. If you have worked with children or young people outside of school settings, such as camps, Sunday school, or scouting, always include those experiences and your responsibilities with the activities. You will want to include other jobs that you have held, especially if they offer a positive insight about your work ethic or abilities. For example, if you worked four summers as a theater cashier, that indicates your longevity to a position.

Adults who have had other careers before moving into the teaching profession will want to summarize those careers on their résumés. For example, selling insurance offers many opportunities to teach people about insurance, indicating that the candidate has people skills and can explain complex policies. Working as a bank cashier probably means that you have good interpersonal skills and can relate to adults. These skills will help you to conduct parent conferences as a teacher. If you have had other jobs, your résumé should not have holes or blanks in terms of employment that you cannot explain. If you took three years off from your bank position to travel the world or stay home with a small child, you do not have to put that on your résumé, but you should be ready to explain those years in a cover letter or interview. Never lie or even embellish on your resume.

Lastly, and very importantly, your résumé must be neat, clear, and easy to read. There should be no typos or misspelled words. Your résumé will be one of your strongest selling points as you look for a job in teaching. Your teaching résumé should be limited to two pages, unless you have a lot of other relevant experience.

YOUR COVER LETTER AND LETTERS OF RECOMMENDATION

When you have located a job opening, you will want to send your résumé with a cover letter to the district advertising the position. The cover letter introduces your résumé and informs the district for which job your application is intended. You should say something in your cover letter about how you learned of this job opening and why you are interested. The cover letter will also state if your letters of recommendation are enclosed with the résumé or if you are having them sent from your college's career center. Your cover letter should summarize how the district can contact you. This letter should be no longer than one page. Obviously, this letter is important and should have good grammar, punctuation, and spelling. Your name should be signed legibly with black ink. Future employers do not want to hire teachers with illegible handwriting, since you will write on students' papers and parents will see your handwriting as well.

The letters of recommendation that you receive should be from professors, your student teaching supervisor, and perhaps most important, from the classroom teacher who served as your cooperating teacher for student teaching. You want the people who write these letters to mention your ability to teach the subject and to manage a classroom, because that is what employers are looking for when they read the letters. If you are entering teaching without having done student teaching or on a provisional certificate without any educational training, your letters should be from former employers who can attest to your work ethic, dependability, perseverance, and ability to work as a team player.

Once you send your cover letter, résumé, and letters of recommendation to a district, you will probably receive a form letter in reply, accompanied by an application specific to that district. You should then complete the application according to the directions on the form, as each application will be different. Some districts require you to have three people complete a checklist recommendation form about you, in addition to your formal letters of recommendation. Any requirements made by the district must be met by you in order to be considered for employment. Remember that you are being judged by the timeliness of returning paperwork, as well as the quality of the paperwork. Always be punctual and accurate with the paperwork if you want to be hired.

TIPS FOR THE JOB FAIR

Your college may have a job fair with prospective employers from school districts early in the spring semester. These recruiters are typically principals, curriculum directors, and personnel directors, all of whom you will work with after you have been hired. Some districts use the job fairs to advertise their schools, giving out lists of vacancies and selling the benefits of living in their town and working in their districts. Other districts actually use the job fair to screen prospective candidates by gathering as many résumés as possible and talking to each candidate for 15 to 20 minutes. They return to their district, sort their notes, and invite top candidates for on-site interviews.

Large school districts have their own job fairs, generally on a Friday or Saturday so that college seniors can attend. At these job fairs, recruiters may be principals, personnel directors, assistant principals, and even classroom teachers. More personnel may be at this fair because the district wants to interview candidates carefully, eliminating follow-up interviews. Contracts may even be extended at this type of job fair. Attending job fairs will give you a very good idea of what the market is like in your area, and it will give you excellent practice in interviewing.

You should never feel pressured to sign a contract or letter of intent at a job fair. If a district needs you so badly, you should be asking yourself, "Why?" The district should give you time to consider the offer, and then set a cut-off date for the return of the contract. The same is true for on-site interviews in school districts.

INTERVIEWS ARE IMPORTANT

Most interviews continue to be held at the school or district where you will be employed. Interviews for teachers are usually about an hour in length, so you don't have a lot of time to sell yourself. Unlike in some business settings, interviews for teachers do not include luncheons or dinners. Most candidates are interviewed by the personnel director or by the building principal. You may have a 30-minute interview with each and then be done. Some schools are using teams of teachers to interview candidates. If you are in a specialty field, like foreign language or science, you may be interviewed by the principal for 45 minutes, then interviewed by a teacher about your knowledge of the subject matter for 20 minutes. Some elementary principals use teachers to finish an interview by having the teacher give a tour of the school and ask the candidate about approaches to teaching reading. So, there is some variety in the interview, depending on the school and system.

When it comes to interviewing, there is no such thing as being over-prepared. You should be prepared for introductory questions and ice-breakers, such as "Tell me a little about yourself." Interviewers don't want your life story, but rather a little about you as a student and something about you that makes you stand out. For example, a candidate for a position teaching Spanish may respond to "Tell me about yourself" by saying, "The most interesting thing about me is that I love speaking Spanish and I spent an entire year of college living abroad so that I could speak the language well and understand the culture." A candidate seeking employment as an elementary teacher may say, "I grew up in a family of teachers and I've been teaching in some way since I was 12 years old. I know that sounds silly, but teaching is in my blood." You only get one chance to make a first impression.

A good interviewer will ask you questions specific to teaching your grade level and subject. You should be prepared to talk about the curriculum that is taught for your grade, the most effective methods employed for teaching this area, and how you plan lessons and units. You will definitely be asked about classroom management and discipline. You may be asked for your philosophy of education and some questions may cover how to motivate students. Employers want to know that you are a nice person who has the strength to teach students and the patience to be nice to them. The employer wants to know if you know your subject matter and how to teach it. They want to know if you can manage a classroom and if you can grade and evaluate students fairly. In essence, they want to know if you have mastered the knowledge base of teaching and if you can discuss how to teach school and actually teach school.

BEHAVIOR-BASED INTERVIEWING

Behavior-based interviewing follows the premise that a candidate's past performance is the best predictor of his/her future behavior. Be prepared for behavior-based interview questions, as this style of interviewing technique has spread from the business world to education. Behavior-based questions ask you to tell about times when you have dealt with specific students or incidents and what you learned from your experience. For example, a question such as "How have you written lesson plans in the past?" should elicit a response from you about some specific plans you wrote and implemented in student teaching. A good answer to this question might be, "During two weeks of my student teaching, I planned every lesson for six classes per day of algebra. Each plan showed how I would introduce the new material, get students involved in problem solving, and then how I would review and close the class. I learned to overplan and keep kids busy from bell to bell." An employer who hears this answer knows that this is probably how you will lesson plan after he/she hires you. Other behavior-based interview questions will start with phrases such as, "Tell me about a time when . . ." or "Tell about your experience with. . . ." Some specific questions might be:

- Tell me about a time when a student has disagreed with you or confronted you in front of the class. What did you do?
- Tell me about a class you taught recently that went really well and one that didn't go as well. What was the difference?
- How have you reached out and communicated with parents?
- What can you as a teacher do to help the students who seem to be lost and behind at the beginning of the year?
- There is only so much time in a day. How do you decide how much time to spend on each subject in your curriculum?

The best way to answer behavior-based questions is to describe specific situations that you have experienced, how you acted, the result, and what you learned. Just being able to answer questions clearly and succinctly tells the interviewer that you can explain things well, and much of teaching is explaining. Your eye contact and tone of voice are very important in a job interview, since your voice and eye contact will also help you to maintain a positive classroom environment.

Many interviews end with hypothetical situation questions, such as "What would you do if you saw a student sleeping in the back of your class?" These questions can be answered with the same type of response as a behavior-based question, since the interviewer really wants to know if you have had this experience, what you did in the past, and what you would do in the future.

After the last questions, hypothetical or other, you will be asked if you have questions for the interviewer. This is a good time for you to ask about the support that the school offers new teachers. You may ask about the school's mentoring program, about release time or staff development for new teachers. Be sure and ask how early you may work in your classroom. This indicates that you want to be organized before the students arrive for the first day of class.

Salary schedules for teachers are set annually by the school board or by the state. In many states the teachers' union negotiates the annual salaries. The salary schedule should be discussed with you by the interviewer, or in a short follow-up with the personnel office. Teachers cannot negotiate separate "deals" as is often done in the business world. Be sure that you understand if you are being hired for a specific position, such as third grade in Lincoln elementary, or if you are being hired as a new elementary teacher whose assignment will be determined the first week of school. Even at the high school level, ask about the specific assignment and number of courses. High school assignments vary, and some principals have the freedom to hire new teachers, assigning them specific classes as school begins. One new teacher said that she accepted a job because she was told that her assignment would be three college-bound chemistry classes and two general science classes. This was a very good assignment. When she actually reported for work that fall she was given two general science and three remedial science courses—a very difficult assignment. When she complained, she was told that she her contract said "five science classes." While student enrollments change quickly in some districts and administrators do have difficulty knowing their faculty needs until school starts, try and find out as much as you can about a position and about any possible changes before you sign the contract.

WHAT TO LOOK FOR IN AN EMPLOYER

We sometimes forget that an interview is a two-way street. While we are busy trying to impress the employer with our experience and potential, we should also remember to ask ourselves if this job is the "right match" for us. If you feel that the principal conducting the interviews is only half-listening, or if he/she accepts phone calls and talks with the secretary during your interview, this person may not give you much time as an employee. Meeting the principal and a few teachers can be a real plus in the interview, because you will be working with these people. If they are easy and personable to talk with initially, they will probably continue to be so.

While it is not appropriate to call someone that you do not know who teaches at the school and ask for background information, you may ask people that you do know about the school or its reputation. Again, college professors supervise in most schools, and your cooperating teacher may have insights into neighboring schools and districts. You may want to complete a couple of interviews before making up your mind about a position.

When interviews are over, be sure to send a thank-you note to the potential employer. This note will remind them who you are and will also signal to them that you pay attention to details. A candidate who writes a thank-you note is probably more likely to write notes home to parents, too.

Once you have been offered a teaching position, be sure and accept by the deadline and complete the follow-up paperwork for your contract and insurance. Many schools need official transcripts, a physical exam, a criminal background check, and the completion of insurance paperwork before they can authorize your first paycheck. After all of this work—you will want to get paid!

STARTING THE JOB WITHOUT FULL CERTIFICATION

If you are offered a contract without completion of certification, of student teaching, or without the required teacher education coursework, you need to ascertain every specific requirement before you accept the job. For example, how many courses per semester will you be required to take and how many semesters can you remain employed before you

get full teacher certification? Are any extensions available if you become ill? Will you be excused from evening activities at the school in
order to go to a college campus that offers these courses? Does the
school understand that you may be supervised weekly by a supervisor
from a nearby college? Will parents understand that the college supervisor is in the classroom so often? If teacher certification depends on
passing a final standardized test, how long do you have to pass that
test? Who pays for the test, you or the district? Horror stories abound
of teachers who are hired provisionally, then are released because they
can't complete requirements for certification by cutoff dates. Some districts hire new teachers and tell them up front that they will be fired 90
days into the school year if they do not produce the certification paperwork due for their job. If the new teacher is awaiting test results for certification, this is a big gamble. The safest thing to do is to become certified and then find a teaching position. However, many people can't
afford this financially, and many districts are anxious to hire provisionally or noncertified teachers in order to have a fully staffed school. Be
aware of the opportunities and of the dangers involved when negotiating for a position before you are fully certified.

QUESTIONS/REFLECTIONS

1. Visit the career center of your college or university and find out
   about upcoming job fairs in education. Are special workshops available for you to learn about résumés, cover letters, and interviews?

2. Talk with practicing teachers about their experiences in job interviewing. What is their best advice?

3. If you are student teaching, ask if you can have a mock interview
   with the principal or other administrator in the building.

CHAPTER 9

Succeeding the First Year

Getting your own classroom is indeed a huge thrill. You may get a feeling that you can change the world by just walking into a classroom that is your very own. Remember that feeling and it will help you to succeed the first year of teaching. The first year has its own set of challenges, but your preparation and your attitude will help you survive and thrive.

BEFORE THE FIRST DAY

Every minute of preparation that you put into organizing your classroom and your curriculum before the school year starts will yield benefits. Hopefully, you will have the opportunity to work in your classroom before the new school year begins. You will be bombarded with orientation sessions and back-to-school faculty meetings the week before classes start, so try to work the week before the work days to organize on your own before you get bogged down with a week of day-long meetings. If your school offers faculty meetings followed by work days without students, take advantage of those days.

What should you do? You should find your room and then make sure that you know where the teachers' workroom and restrooms are. Find the students' restrooms as well, and know which hallways are which, so that you can direct lost students on the first day of school. Go back to your classroom and count the students' desks. Compare the number of desks with the number of students on your class rosters and then arrange for more desks if you don't have enough. Do not assume that somebody else will do this, or that the number of desks was even considered when students were assigned to rooms.

Evaluate your room for other needs. You will want an entrance table where students can pick up materials and graded papers as they enter the room. If you have elementary or middle grades students, you will have to organize a place for coats, backpacks, and sack lunches if students do not have lockers like the high school students. You should have an extra table for students to use when they need to find makeup assignments. Have a safe place for your own purse or personal bag. Don't carry much cash or credit cards to work with you.

Look at the room and think about traffic patterns, then arrange the desks, chairs, and tables. Make sure that you have room to walk in between aisles, because proximity to the students is a good deterrent of minor behavior problems. Sit in the students' desks and make sure that you can see the board, the television, and the projection screen.

Check on the availability of computers and projectors. Will some equipment be assigned to your room or will you have to check out machines ahead of time? What is available for you to make bulletin boards and other posters? Where do you get materials for art or science projects? Your assigned mentor will probably answer these questions for you. In some districts the new teacher and his/her mentor are paid for two or three extra work days before faculty meetings begin. Paid or unpaid, these days can be lifesavers. Many times the toughest part of organizing is simply finding who to ask for supplies and when and how to requisition what you need. Keep asking questions and you will get answers! Don't buy anything yourself until you know what the school provides. It is very helpful to have facial tissues and adhesive bandages in your room, in addition to extra pencils, markers, tape, and other teaching supplies.

More important than bulletin boards, you need to make sure that your name is posted clearly on the door and that students' names or your rosters are also posted. Students are terrified of being in the wrong room on the first day of school. You will also want to post the school's rules and your classroom rules before the first day of class. Find out emergency procedures in case of fire, tornado, or student violence.

You will need to do some long-range planning before the students arrive, too. You may plan with other teachers in your grade or subject area because texts and readers need to be shared. If you are part of a teaching team, you may spend several days mapping out the year's curriculum before the students arrive. Create fairly detailed plans for the first few days and then you will be ready to actually meet the students. Have a few extra activities ready to keep students busy if the initial days of school have an irregular schedule due to hot days, broken air conditioning, or pull-out programs for health testing.

THE VERY FIRST DAY

Get yourself organized personally before the first day. Plan to be at home the evening before and to go to bed early. After your good night's sleep, eat a healthy breakfast and get to work a little early. Dress professionally—you have only one chance to make a good first impression on your students. High school students don't really want a teacher who dresses as they do. Even second graders know what a real teacher should look like.

It is very important that you know at least one teacher next door or across the hall. Should a major question or crisis arise, you can run to this person in between classes to ask your question.

When the students arrive, greet them. Stand at the door, direct them to go in, find a seat, and begin the assignment on the board for their class. You may even want to shake hands with your students! Many teachers put the child's name on the seat (elementary school) and direct children to their own place. In middle and high school, put the seating chart on the overhead projector and let students know that they need to find their seat based on your chart. Your organization sets the tone for the first day, the first week, and even the first year. Don't hesitate to make seating charts—the most organized, effective teachers do.

The assignment on the board should be one requesting information that you really need. For example, ask middle school students to fill out a card with their favorite books, movies, television shows, and all-time favorite food. If you need information cards with parent/guardian numbers, this can be your first assignment. When the bell rings and you enter the room, get the students' attention and let them know what they will do for the rest of the day or hour. Take charge in a caring, humane way, but take charge. Be prepared for some students to talk out or resist initial assignments, no matter how simple. Be prepared for dealing with student stress, which may even be higher than your own on the first day of school. In elementary school, young children have even been known to throw up on the first day of school from high stress. That's why you need to know the custodian and how to reach him/her.

You will want to introduce yourself and the subject(s) to be taught. Let students introduce themselves, too. Teach basic rules and have students complete some type of activity or assignment. Reading a book is great for elementary. One demonstration or problem-solving activity will hook the interest of older students. Before the students leave your class, remind them of what they learned and what they need for the next day. Teach the students what you expect them to bring to class each and every day. When you dismiss the class, smile and breathe! Always make notes in your plan book about the class and length of activities. The better your notes, the smoother the next class and the next year.

BEST TIPS FOR MANAGEMENT

You must begin planning for classroom management before the students ever enter your room. Go back to texts discussed in your training, or to ones presented in this book, and make a classroom management plan that you present to students the very first day. Students may have input, or even be the ones who word the rules, but you must be the guide and leader for your rules. Rules need to be posted and distributed to students and parents during the first week of school. Remember to have positives and consequences for your rules. If a student breaks a rule, you must be ready to reinforce the rule with a consequence, so make the rules realistic, observable, and enforceable. See Canter's and Wong's works to make your management plan a workable one.

Your voice, your professional clothing, your sense of confidence, and the arrangement of the furniture in the classroom will all contribute to good management. Do not be a teacher who says, "I didn't like the rules and I'm not going to start with them. I'll just tell the kids I'm different and I'm their friend and we'll only worry about rules if they start misbehaving." Students want and need parameters for their classroom behavior. Be prepared and be organized. Be the adult, not their buddy. Yes, you can show genuine friendship and caring, but you have been hired to be the professional educator. You will need to manage the classroom in order to educate the students.

Good management also includes reviewing rules and policies when a new week begins. You will definitely need to review the rules after the first long weekend, Thanksgiving, and holiday breaks. Many of your students may live with one parent during the week and a second parent on the weekends. Grandparents may take the children over special breaks. While some students handle these situations with grace, the stress shows on other children. For some of your students, you and your classroom may be the most stable, consistent environment they experience. Settling the class and using routines will make all of your management strategies easier.

Above all else, seek help when needed. Some students may need individual behavior contracts in order to work well in your room. A special education teacher or counselor should be able to help you with these contracts. Many teachers realize that one child is changing the entire environment for the whole class. Is it fair to let one child's behavior change the learning experiences for 27 others? However, when you seek help with management and behavior, you may be told that the students are your responsibility. If that is the case, keep trying plans that work for you and the students. Management improves as the students realize that you are the caring professional who wants them to succeed. Management does take time. Always being prepared with meaningful lessons may be the best guide to maintaining good management. If the students know that they come into your class and work at something important from bell to bell, they will respond.

COMMUNICATION IS THE KEY

Good, clear communication with parents, colleagues, administrators, and the students is truly the key for a successful year. Begin with an introductory letter home to parents the first week of class. Let parents know the class rules and how much important learning will be going on. Be specific, telling parents that their child will be learning the alphabet, or how to speak French, or how to solve advanced math formulas. And yes, letters home to parents are not just the responsibility of elementary teachers. Letters home in middle school and high school are important. You may want to write a short month-long syllabus for older students, and send a copy home to parents with a short paragraph for them attached. Let parents know your office hours or preparation time and how to reach you during that time. You may need to stress that you are teaching six classes a day and cannot return calls until a certain time of the day.

Some teachers tell me that they know that letters they send home with students never get home. We all know this to be true. However, we should still send letters home. At some point in our careers, we come to realize that we may not reach every child, but we have to try to reach students and their parents. Keep a file of your letters to parents, trying to write one every grading period. If a parent comes in for a conference, refer back to your letters and syllabi sent to them earlier in the year. Being able to document your efforts and being able to document student work will be a tremendous help in these parent conferences. If a parent says, "I've never received anything and didn't know this," you can take the opportunity to suggest that they talk more with their child about these papers and schoolwork in general. Maybe the parent can leave self-addressed, stamped envelopes for future newsletters to be mailed home.

Being clear with the students and their parents is important, and communicating with your colleagues and administrators is the next step for a successful year. When you send a newsletter home, make sure that your building administrators get a copy. You may have a curriculum director, an assistant principal, and a principal. Keep them all informed until you see that some really do not need the information. Document your work in a portfolio so that when you are evaluated by your administrators, you can talk about student activities and successes that they might not have seen when visiting your class. If your administrator does not clarify how you will be evaluated, ask about the process. You may want to ask a veteran teacher to observe one of your lessons prior to the evaluator's visit, just to get feedback from a colleague.

Now, just how do you communicate with colleagues and become part of the team? This is actually easier in some schools than others. Some schools allow time for joint planning for teachers of the same grade or subject. Whether time is scheduled or not, make every effort to meet and talk with other teachers about curriculum. Keep informed about what is going on in the grades preceding and following yours. Support other teachers by attending games, plays, and extra-curricular events.

Be very careful about taking students out of another teacher's class for a field trip, early release for sports, or other reason. As teachers, we are very possessive of our time and we know that time on task equates to more learning. If an event or trip requires you to take students from another teacher, always ask well in advance. It is always necessary, and important politically, to get administrative support prior to asking teachers to release students for extra events. The school should have clear policies about such releases. Learn the school's policies early and realize that as the new teacher you can't make a lot of changes to policies overnight.

Do the teachers have cliques just as the students do? They may, and that may be the reason that some new teachers make a point to join in the teachers' lounge while others stay away from the lounge completely. You will have to get to know your colleagues and decide where you fit. The important things to remember about joining a school faculty are basically the same pieces of advice to remember anytime you start a new job. Respect the other teachers. Listen to them, but make your own decisions. Don't get involved in gossip. Smile and be courteous and just do all the things we know are common sense and good judgment.

STRESS MANAGEMENT FOR YOU

Some stress is good for you. It motivates you to write innovative plans and to get up early in the morning and start your day. However, when most people hear the word stress, they immediately think of the dangers of too much stress in their lives, since stress is a contributing factor for major medical problems. We have all experienced temporary stress that kept us from sleeping, made us crave and eat junk food, or drained us of energy from too much worry.

Teaching is often listed as one of the more stressful careers in modern society. Learning to cope and deal with the stress of teaching is an important lesson for all teachers. The first step in dealing with stress is recognizing that you are stressed and identifying specific stressors of the job. Many teachers say that large class sizes create stress, or that the constant pace and noise of the school are stressful. Some teachers report that just worrying about all the parent complaints and the community's pressure to have an excellent school gives them stress. While symptoms of stress may vary from headaches to loss of sleep to weight gain, you will probably know when you are stressed. What do you do about your stress and how can you lower the stress or create coping mechanisms?

Taking care of your physical health is vitally important in stress management. You have to eat a healthy, balanced diet and watch your intake of caffeine, high-sugar foods, and alcohol. This may be hard if the only snacks at teachers' meetings are coffee and doughnuts! Carry your apple or banana and a diet caffeine-free soda if healthy snacks aren't provided at meetings. Packing a sack lunch may be the only way to get a lunch and have five minutes of free time over your lunch hour.

Many teachers find ways to create minutes of "down time" during the day. You may have to come to school 15 minutes early to prepare for your classes in order to take 10 minutes of free time during your preparation hour. Use that time for a cup of herbal tea and prop your feet up with the door to your classroom closed for just a few minutes.

Exercise is another excellent stress buster. I used to walk to and from school to ensure getting a 40-minute walk in every day. I know other teachers who take advantage of working at a school by shooting hoops in the gym or using the weight room when classes are over. Some teachers swim and others jog. Ask those health and physical education teachers what they recommend and they will say exercise.

I once attended a stress management seminar where the speaker began by asking us to raise our hand if we always brushed our teeth every day. Obviously, every hand in the room went up. She then asked us how many of us planned stress management time daily, with the same regularity with which we brushed our teeth. Few hands went up. The point of this story is that we must plan and organize ourselves and our busy days so that we have some time each day for exercise and/or unwinding. I know some women who take bubble baths as their top stress management routine. Others set time aside two nights a week for their favorite sitcoms on television. Reward yourself with a magazine, some time for a romance novel, or a walk through the neighborhood.

The key to stress management is different for every individual. Each teacher must find his/her own stress busters and ways of unwinding. Some people love to garden and find it very restful. I find that gardening increases my stress. Rather than garden, I make sure that I walk for two miles every day. I also knew a teacher who kept a bag of chocolates in her desk. After the students left, she ate just one chocolate, then made sure her lesson plans were ready for the next day. When the plans were ready, she left the building and concentrated on cooking a nice meal for her family, which was a stress reliever for her. Every person's plan will be different, but we should each have something that we do for stress relief.

Taking a walk or reading will not take away the problems that exist in the classroom. If a problem persists and overwhelms us, such as dealing with several behavior-disorder students in one class or being unable to raise test scores with a certain class, then we should find a way to confront the problem and get help from the school administration, counselors, and fellow teachers. Throughout your teaching career you will be confronted with serious challenges and concerns. You will probably not be able to resolve every problem successfully. Taking care of yourself physically and finding the balance between work and relaxation will enable you to cope more successfully with problems and with the stresses that come from teaching.

FINDING THE BALANCE

There are some weeks when teachers find themselves at school three nights out of five and are still grading papers and writing plans on Sunday evening. Some Saturdays you will find yourself working with students or attending a conference about a new teaching strategy. Even during calm weeks you will be busy with planning and coordinating the academic programs of all of your students. Teaching is a demanding and challenging profession and it often feels that the work never ends. However, there will be other times that balance the stress of the busiest work weeks.

I was running an errand at the mall last week and saw one of my former students who is now an elementary teacher. He was walking in the mall with his wife and three small children. When I asked how his school year had gone, he replied, "It was good—challenging, but good. The best part of the school year is right now, because now I am with my own kids for the next eight weeks." He obviously balances his work with his desire to spend a lot of time with his own children and finds that teaching allows him to do this.

I have known some teachers who choose to teach part-time for decades because that is what works for them. Others choose substitute teaching as a permanent job for several years while their own children are small. Some teachers work full-time and tell me that their jobs are better because they know that they will not be on-call during weekends and holidays as some of their friends in nursing and business are. My own sister-in-law gets either Thanksgiving or Christmas off, but never both, since she is a surgical nurse in a small hospital. My brother often works on the Fourth of July. Teachers are always off for these and other holidays. While teaching takes a lot of time and energy, it is a still a profession where balance is possible and time off is significantly longer than other jobs.

QUESTIONS/REFLECTIONS

1. Plan to work with a teacher for three days before the school year starts and then plan to observe that teacher on the first day of school. What does he/she do to get the classroom organized? How does the first day of school go for the teacher? For the students?

2. Prepare a folder with extra activities for the first few days of school for the grade level that you plan to teach. Each time you see a good activity in a field experience, write a note card about it so that you can replicate the activity when you start teaching.

3. Ask a practicing teacher for his/her best hints for classroom management and discipline. What have been the biggest challenges that these teachers have experienced?

4. Ask a teacher what he/she does to unwind and manage stress. Would his/her activities work for you? Why or why not?

CHAPTER 10

Advice from Other Teachers

When my graduate students found out I was writing a book to help people decide if they wanted to be teachers, they asked if they could write letters to the readers of the book and tell them why they should (or should not) consider teaching as a profession. These students were practicing teachers who ranged in experience from one to 21 years in the classroom.

The following excerpts are from the letters my students wrote. All wanted to remain anonymous, but some wanted their field of teaching and years of experience noted. The excerpts show the positives and the negatives of teaching. The teachers' thoughts are genuine and heartfelt, indicating that while teaching is a love and a passion, it is also a challenge like no other. I hope their thoughts help you as you consider the profession of teaching.

MUSIC TEACHER, 21 YEARS OF EXPERIENCE

When you consider becoming a teacher, you are taking responsibility for the future of humanity. The information you share will impact and influence generations to come. The social skills that are modeled in your class will likely have a global influence as technology continues to unfold.

Should you decide to teach make sure that you are firmly grounded in what you believe. Be receptive to new approaches and strategies of teaching, but always let your students feel secure in your position of what you teach, how you present it, and maintain your classroom discipline.

Never forget the big picture of how the student will apply what he is learning. Help the student keep things in perspective. Laugh, cry, play—and love the children no matter what!

I never dreamed that I would teach. In hindsight, my career has been a comedy of errors, yet I am most blessed because I have ended up as the music teacher at our school. I have a job that I love and a position with reasonable work hours that provides time for my family.

Life is a trade-off and your time is your most precious commodity. Are you willing to dedicate your time to influence the future for your children and grandchildren? Your decision has real consequences!

KINDERGARTEN TEACHER, TWO YEARS OF EXPERIENCE

So I hear you are considering the profession. Would you like the good or the bad news first? If you chose good, keep reading. If you chose the bad, just remember that all professions have their ups and downs. Now back to the good.

I cannot imagine getting up every morning and not going to work in my classroom. Teaching is very time-consuming and stressful, but it is by far the most rewarding profession. At the kindergarten level, you get to see all the light bulbs (when teachers refer to light bulbs, they usually mean that they can sense when a student has learned something, because it is as if a light bulb has popped on over the student's head) and smiling faces all day long. Yes, there are the students that will drive you up the wall all day long, but the minute they bug you, just look at all of the other students to remind you of the importance of your profession.

Just remember to look past everything you will have to do as a teacher and all of the mounds of paperwork (no, is doesn't matter how many organizers you have, you will never be organized) and look to the children. Every day is a new day and start it with a clean slate.

FOURTH-GRADE TEACHER, THREE YEARS OF EXPERIENCE

I was in the business world for 10 years before I left to become a teacher. I have never worked as hard at something. Your hours are long (9½ a day) and you get very little "relief" time. The rewards, however, are great. The satisfaction that you have taught a student well, that you have "hit home" and the light bulb has come on, is terrific. To know that you are important to 25 little lives for an entire year is awesome. To be able to change a mood or an entire attitude of a student with a smile or a kind word is power.

It's nice to be able to control your day. You are basically in charge of your room. You can be highly creative and have fun while getting paid for it. You have time off when your own children do and summers free. I don't care what anyone says, but the pay is not that bad for only working 180 days a year. You better love being with children or it will seem unbearable.

THIRD-GRADE TEACHER, 11 YEARS OF EXPERIENCE

Teaching is the most consuming job I've ever had. I worked for the phone company for 10 years before entering teaching and I was never as passionate about it as I am teaching. At the phone company I was an employee that held down a job from 8 A.M. to 5 P.M. Now I am a teacher 24 hours a day, seven days a week, nine months of the year. Every relationship I have is influenced by teaching. My way of thinking is influenced by teaching. Teaching just isn't a job, it's a lifestyle. So, if you want a lifelong mission, a life of complete work and satisfaction, then teach.

HIGH SCHOOL MATH TEACHER, FIVE YEARS OF EXPERIENCE

Teaching is a very fulfilling profession, but it is not for everyone. Teaching requires a tremendous amount of energy, patience, passion for the subject you teach, excellent people and political skills, and most important, a great love for children. Since teachers deal with children and adolescents, each day is different. Just when you think you have figured out a class, they change on you! You never know what kind of situation a child is coming from when they get to school, so each child is different as well.

I love teaching, but it does wear me out, not only physically, but emotionally as well. I don't think I would enjoy an office job, because I love the spontaneity of the students and the feeling of making a difference in their lives. Plus, kids are extremely funny at times, so you must have a good sense of humor. You really never know what to expect.

FIFTH-GRADE TEACHER, FOUR YEARS OF EXPERIENCE

One must understand that teaching is not simply the transmission of information from one person to another. It is much, much more. A teacher must know how to transmit the information in a manner that is appropriate for each child. A teacher must be prepared to understand each student's psychological profile. A teacher must be willing to delve into the world of each child's background. A teacher must be ready to counsel when needed. Then, and only then, can a teacher organize a lesson plan.

Summer vacation, holidays, and spring break are wonderful mental breaks. The salary is not terrible. My heart is in teaching and everyday is a day worth waking up for. This job is for the hard working, caring, inspired individual.

THIRD-GRADE TEACHER, THREE YEARS OF EXPERIENCE

My advice to someone who is undecided about becoming a teacher is to tell them that teaching is a calling. It is something you have to do. The job is very demanding. A teacher never has enough hours in a day to get done what needs to be done to give the students the best education. Education for a teacher is also never finished. You will always be in school after you do your work in the classroom. Your pay is already very low but you will end up spending a great deal of it to buy your own teaching supplies. You will never have the answer to why do I do all of this except to say, "I have to." And yes, you do have to, because it is your calling.

ART TEACHER, EIGHT YEARS OF EXPERIENCE

I worked as a graphic designer/illustrator before I decided to add teacher certification to my undergraduate degree. I have never regretted this decision.

Every job I have chosen has been fulfilling, but teaching is the most fulfilling and the most challenging. One needs to be capable of making split-second decisions. One has to be flexible, firm, and caring. One must be prepared and capable of setting goals and sticking to them. A teacher needs to be able to look at the whole picture and break it into pieces before deciding how to plan the curriculum. One might have to change the shape of several pieces in order to make them fit.

A teacher never gives up and always keeps things new to improve his/her teaching. If you have these qualities, you will probably be a good teacher.

SECOND-GRADE TEACHER, 20 YEARS OF EXPERIENCE

Things have changed so much in the 20 years that I have been teaching. I don't know that I would actually recommend to someone to become a teacher. Every year more and more is added to our plates. You have so many skills and programs that you have to teach. It is often frustrating because I feel like I am unable to teach things thoroughly or for mastery. Now, more than ever, teachers are going to be held accountable for their students' test scores. That is more added pressure.

The process for getting help for students who might have learning and/or behavior problems is often frustrating. The paperwork and meetings are often too many, and it sometimes takes a year or longer to get help for students.

The diversity of student abilities, performance, and behavior make for many challenges every day. So much time during the day is spent redirecting off-task behaviors, problem solving, and dealing with interruptions that you often feel like you haven't had an opportunity to teach.

HIGH SCHOOL MATH TEACHER

The disadvantages of teaching are profound. I think my biggest complaint is that I am not treated as a professional. We have so many constraints placed on us and so many people telling us what exactly we are doing wrong that it is disheartening most times. The paperwork increases every year. The number of roles that I am expected to perform increases exponentially. How am I supposed to accomplish everything? One word describes this: frustration.

However, as bad as it gets sometimes, there is magic in knowing that you have had an effect on at least one child. And for me, there is great satisfaction in witnessing a student's successful performance because of something that I have taught. One of the best compliments I've ever received happened just yesterday. My fourth-period class sent me a dozen roses and said, "thank you." If they can look back on their high school career and at least have one pleasant memory of geometry (along with obviously having learned geometry) then I have succeeded.

SECOND-GRADE TEACHER, FOUR YEARS OF EXPERIENCE

I would first ask them if they are truly willing to do whatever it takes to help a child. I would tell them not to get into teaching if they wanted to only work from 7 to 3. I would tell them not to get into teaching if they are going to be negative consistently. I had no idea how important it was to get into a school that has a great administration. You must be at a school where you are supported by your principal.

I would tell them to be very careful what they say to their coworkers. I would tell them to document everything and be ready to have a conference with an upset parent.

I would tell them to think long and hard about this decision. Do they want to teach to change lives? Can they live off the salary they will make? I would ask that person not to do it if they only want to teach for summers and holidays off. Get into teaching if you are ready to be taught some of life's greatest lessons. Get into teaching if you want to have each day be a new beginning. Get into teaching if you want to help children see the positive impact that learning can have. Get into teaching if you want to be a role model. Get into teaching if you want to reach a child who is unreachable. Get into teaching if you want to leave a legacy.

Teacher Certification Offices

(Source: American Association for Employment in Education's 2000 *Job Search Handbook for Educators*, pages 41–42. See the source for more information about which states require exams and tests.)

ALABAMA
Department of Education
Division of Instructional Service
5108 Gordon Persons Building
50 North Ripley Street
Montgomery 36130-2101, 334-242-9977

ALASKA
Department of Education
Teacher Education and Certification
Goldbelt Building
801 West 10th Street, Suite 200
Juneau 99801-1894, 907-465-2831
www.educ.state.ak.us/teachercertification

ARIZONA
Department of Education
Teacher Certification Unit
P.O. Box 6490
1535 West Jefferson
Phoenix 85005-6490, 602-542-4367
www.ade.state.az.us/certification

ARKANSAS
Department of Education
Teacher Education and Licensure
#4 State Capitol Mall, Rooms 106B/107B
Little Rock 72201, 501-682-4342
www.state.ar.us/ade

CALIFORNIA
Commission on Teacher Credentialing
1900 Capital Avenue
Sacramento 95814-4213, 916-445-0184
www.ctc.ca.gov

COLORADO
Department of Education
Educator Licensing, Room 105
201 East Colfax Avenue
Denver 80203-1799, 303-866-6628
www.cde.state.co.us

CONNECTICUT
State Department of Education
Bureau of Certification and Teacher Preparation
P.O. Box 2219
Hartford 06145-2219, 860-566-5201
www.state.ct.us/sde

DELAWARE
State Department of Education
Office of Certification
Townsend Building
P.O. Box 1402
Dover 19903-1402, 302-739-4686
www.doe.state.de.us

DISTRICT OF COLUMBIA
Teacher Education and Certification Branch
Main Administration Building
825 N. Capitol Street, NE, 6th Floor
Washington, DC 20002, 202-442-5377

FLORIDA
Department of Education
Bureau of Teacher Certification
Rath Turlington Building
325 West Gaines Street, Room 203
Tallahassee 32399-0400, 850-488-5724
www.firn.edu/doe/6a-4.htm

GEORGIA
Professional Standards Commission
1454 Twin Towers East
Atlanta 30334, 404-657-9000
www.gapsc.com

HAWAII
State Department of Education
Personnel & Certification Management
P.O. Box 2360
Honolulu 96804, 808-586-3265
www.k12.hi.us

IDAHO
Department of Education
Teacher Certification and Professional Standards
P.O. Box 83720
Boise 83720-0027, 208-332-6884
www.sde.state.id.us/certification

ILLINOIS
State Teacher Certification Board
100 North First Street
Springfield 62777-0001, 217-782-2805
www.isbe.state.il.us/homepage.html

INDIANA
Professional Standards Board
251 East Ohio Street, Suite 201
Indianapolis 46204-2133, 317-232-9010
www.state.in.us/psb/

IOWA
Board of Education Examiners
Teacher Licensure
Grimes State Office Building
East 14th and Grand
Des Moines 50319-0146, 515-281-3245
www.state.ia.us/educate/depteduc/elseced/praclic/license/index.html

KANSAS
State Department of Education
Certification and Teacher Education
120 SE 10th Avenue
Topeka 66612-1182, 785-296-2288
www.ksbe.state.ks.us/cert/cert.html

KENTUCKY
Office of Teacher Education and Certification
1024 Capitol Center Drive
Frankfort 40601, 502-573-4606
www.kde.state.ky.us

LOUISIANA
State Department of Education
Certification and Higher Education
626 North 4th Street
P.O. Box 94064
Baton Rouge 70804-9064, 225-342-3490
www.doe.state.la.us

MAINE
Department of Education
Certification Office
23 State House Station
Augusta 04333-0023, 207-287-5944
www.state.me.us

MARYLAND
State Department of Education
Certification Branch
200 West Baltimore Street

Baltimore 21201-2595, 410-767-0412
www.msde.state.md.us

MASSACHUSETTS
Department of Education
Certification and Professional Development Coordination
350 Main Street, P.O. Box 9140
Malden 02148-5023, 781-388-3300 ext. 665
www.info.doe.mass.edu/news.html

MICHIGAN
Department of Education
Office of Professional Preparation and Certification Services
608 West Allegan, 3rd Floor
Lansing 48909, 517-373-3310
www.mde.state.mi.us

MINNESOTA
State Department of Children, Families & Learning
Personnel Licensing
1500 Hwy. 36 West
Roseville 55113, 651-582-8691
www.cfl.state.mn.us

MISSISSIPPI
State Department of Education
Educator Licensure
P.O. Box 771
Jackson 39205-0771, 601-359-3483
http://mdek12.state.ms.us

MISSOURI
Department of Elementary & Secondary Education
Teacher Certification Section
205 Jefferson Street
P.O. Box 480
Jefferson City 65102-0480, 573-751-0051
http://services.dese.state.mo.us

MONTANA
Office of Public Instruction
Teacher Education and Certification
P.O. Box 202501
Helena 59620-2501, 406-444-3150
www.metnet.state.mt.us

NEBRASKA
Department of Education
Teacher Education and Certification
301 Centennial Mall South, Box 94987
Lincoln 68509-4987, 402-471-0739
http://edneb.org

NEVADA
Department of Education
Licensure Division
700 East 5th Street
Carson City 89701, 775-687-9115
www.nsn.k12.nv.us/nvdoe

NEW HAMPSHIRE
State Department of Education
Bureau of Credentialing
101 Pleasant Street
Concord 03301-3860, 603-271-2407
www.state.nh.us/doe/education.htm

NEW JERSEY
Department of Education
Office of Licensing
Riverview Executive Plaza,
Building 100, Rte. 29
Trenton 08625-0500, 609-292-2045

NEW MEXICO
State Department of Education
Professional Licensure Unit
Education Building
Santa Fe 87501-2786, 505-827-6587
www.sde.state.nm.us

NEW YORK
State Education Department
Office of Teaching
Albany 12234, 518-474-3901
www.nysed.gov/tcert/homepage/htm

NORTH CAROLINA
Department of Public Instruction
Licensure Section
301 North Wilmington Street
Raleigh 27601-2825, 919-733-4125
www.dpi.state.nc.us

NORTH DAKOTA
Education Standards Practices Board
600 East Boulevard Avenue,
Dept. 202
Bismarck 58505-0080, 701-328-2264

OHIO
Department of Education
Division of Professional Development and Licensure
65 South Front Street, Room 412
Columbus 43215-4183, 614-466-3593
www.ode.ohio.gov/www/tc/teacher.html

OKLAHOMA
State Department of Education
Professional Standards Section
Hodge Education Building
2500 North Lincoln Boulevard, Room 212
Oklahoma City 73105-4599, 405-521-3337
www.sde.state.ok.us

OREGON
Teacher Standards and Practices Commission
Public Service Building, Suite 105
255 Capitol Street, NE
Salem 97310-1332, 503-378-3586
www.ode.state.or.us/tspc

PENNSYLVANIA
State Department of Education
Bureau of Teacher Certification & Preparation
333 Market Street, 3rd Floor
Harrisburg 17126-0333, 717-787-3356
www.pde.psu.edu

PUERTO RICO
Department of Education
Certification Office
P.O. Box 190759
San Juan 00919-0759, 787-753-9128

RHODE ISLAND
Department of Education
Office of Teacher Preparation, Certification, and Professional Development
Shepard Building
255 Westminster Street
Providence 02903, 401-222-2675

SOUTH CAROLINA
State Department of Education
Office of Teacher Education, Certification & Evaluation
1600 Gervais Street
Columbia 29201, 803-734-8466
www.state.sc.us/sde/commques/certcont.htm

SOUTH DAKOTA
Department of Education & Cultural Affairs
Office of Policy and Accountability
Kneip Building, 700 Governors Drive
Pierre 57501-2291, 605-773-3553
www.state.sd.us/state/executive/deca/account/certif.htm

TENNESSEE
State Department of Education
Teacher Licensing and Certification
Andrew Johnson Tower, 5th Floor
710 James Robertson Parkway

Nashville 37243-0377, 615-532-4885
www.state.tn.us/education/lic-home.htm

TEXAS
State Board for Educator Certification
1001 Trinity Street
Austin 78701-2603, 512-469-3001
www.sbec.state.tx.us

UTAH
State Office of Education
Educator Licensing
250 East 500 South
Salt Lake City 84111, 801-538-7500
www.usoe.k12.ut.us/cert/reqs.html

VERMONT
State Department of Education
Licensing & Professional Standards
120 State Street
Montpelier 05620, 802-828-2445
www.state.vt.us/educ

VIRGINIA
Department of Education
James Monroe Building
P.O. Box 2120
Richmond 23218-2120, 804-371-2522
www.pen.k12.va.us/Anthology/VDOE/Compliance/TeachEd

WASHINGTON
Superintendent of Public Instruction
Professional Education and Certification Office
Old Capitol Building
P.O. Box 47200
Olympia 98504-7200, 360-753-6773
www.k12.wa.us

WEST VIRGINIA
Department of Education

Office of Professional Preparation
1900 Kanawha Boulevard East
Building #6, Room B-252
Charleston 25305-0330, 304-558-7010
www.wvde.state.wv.us

WISCONSIN
Department of Public Instruction
Teacher Education & Licensing Teams
125 South Webster Street, P.O. Box 7841
Madison 53707-7841, 608-266-1879
www.dp.state.wi.us/dpi/jbsintro.html

WYOMING
Professional Teaching Standards Board
Hathaway Building, 2nd Floor
2300 Capitol Avenue
Cheyenne 82002-0190, 307-777-6248
www.k12.wy.us

Bibliography

American Association for Employment in Education (AAEE). (2000). *2000 Job search handbook for educators*. Columbus, OH: author.

Armstrong, D. G., Henson, K. T., & Savage, T. V. (1997). *Teaching today: An introduction to education*. Upper Saddle River, NJ: Merrill.

Burden, P. R. (1995). *Classroom management and discipline*. White Plains, NY: Longman.

Callahan, J. F., Clark, L. H., & Kellough, R. D. (1998). *Teaching in the middle and secondary schools* (6th ed.). Upper Saddle River, NJ: Merrill/ Prentice-Hall.

Canter, L., & Canter, M. (1992). *Assertive discipline*. Santa Monica, CA: Lee Canter.

Canter, L., & Canter, M. (1993). *Succeeding with difficult students*. Santa Monica, CA: Lee Canter.

Canter, L., & Canter, M. (1995). *Behavior management in the middle school classroom*. Santa Monica, CA: Lee Canter.

Charles, C. M. (1999). *Building classroom discipline* (6th ed.). New York: Longman.

Clement, M. C. (2000). *Building the best faculty: Strategies for hiring and supporting new teachers*. Lanham, MD: Scarecrow Press.

Clement, M. C., Enz, B. J., & Pawlas, G. E. (2000). The apprentice teacher. In B. E. Steffy, M. P. Wolfe, S. H. Pasch, & B. J. Enz (Eds.) *Life cycle of the career teacher*. Thousand Oaks, CA: Corwin.

Cruikshank, D. R., Bainer, D., & Metcalf, K. (1995). *The act of teaching*. New York: McGraw-Hill.

Davidman, L., & Davidman, P. T. (2001). *Teaching with a multicultural perspective*. New York: Longman.

Dollase, R. H. (1992). *Voices of beginning teachers: Visions and realities*. New York: Teachers College Press.

Duarte, E. M., & Smith, S. (2000). *Foundational perspectives in multicultural education*. New York: Longman.

Farkas, Johnson, & Foleno. (2000). *A sense of calling: Who teaches and why.* New York: Public Agenda.

Fuery, C. (1990). *Are you still teaching? A survival guide to keep you sane.* Captiva Island, FL: Sanibel Sanddollar Publications.

Gordan, S. P. (1991). *How to help beginning teachers succeed.* Alexandria, VA: Association for Supervision and Curriculum Development.

Haberman, M. (1995). *Star teachers of children in poverty.* West Lafayette, IN: Kappa Delta Pi.

Henson, K. T., & Eller, B. (1999). *Educational psychology for effective teaching.* Belmont, CA: Wadsworth.

Igoa, C. (1995). *The inner world of the immigrant child.* Mahwah, NJ: Lawrence Erlbaum.

Kantrowitz, B., & Wingert, P. (2000, October 2). Teachers wanted. *Newsweek, 136*(14), 36–42.

Kellough, R. D., & Kellough, N. G. (1999). *Secondary school teaching: A guide to methods and resources: Planning for success.* Upper Saddle River, NJ: Merrill.

McNeil, J. D. (1999). *Curriculum: The teacher's initiative* (2nd ed.). Upper Saddle River, NJ: Merrill.

Moore, K. D. (1995). *Classroom teaching skills* (3rd ed.). New York: McGraw-Hill.

Morrison, G. S. (1997). *Teaching in America.* Boston: Allyn and Bacon.

National Commission on Teaching & America's Future. (1996). *What matters most: Teaching for America's future.* New York: Teachers College.

Nieto, S. (2000). *Affirming diversity* (3rd ed.). New York: Longman.

Orlich, D. C., Harder, R. J., Callahan, R. C., Kauchak, D. P., Pendergrass, R. A., Keogh, A. J., & Gibson, H. (1990). *Teaching strategies: A guide to better instruction* (3rd ed.). Lexington, MA: D. C. Heath.

Parkay, F. W., & Hardcastle Stanford, B. (1998). *Becoming a teacher* (4th ed.). Boston: Allyn & Bacon.

Ryan, K., & Cooper, J. M. (1998). *Those who can, teach* (8th ed.). Boston: Houghton Mifflin.

Schurr, S. L., Thomason, J., & Thomason, M. (1995). *Teaching at the middle level.* Lexington, MA: DC Heath.

Southworth, S. A. (2000). Wanted: Two million teachers. *Instructor, 109*(5), 25–27.

Steffy, B. E. (1989). *Career stages of classroom stages.* Lancaster, PA: Technomic.

Steffy, B. E., Wolfe, M. E., Pasch, S. H., & Enz, B. J. (Eds.). (2000). *Life cycle of the career teacher.* Thousand Oaks, CA: Corwin.

Tauber, R. T. (1995). *Classroom management: Theory and practice.* Fort Worth: Harcourt Brace College Publishers.

Travers, P. D., & Rebore, R. W. (2000). *Foundations of education: Becoming a teacher* (4th ed.). Boston: Allyn & Bacon.

Veenman, S. (1984). Perceived problems of beginning teachers. *Review of Educational Research, 54*(2), 143–178.

Weinstein, C. S. (1996). *Secondary classroom management.* Boston: McGraw-Hill.

Weinstein, C. S., & Mignano A. J., Jr. (1993). *Elementary classroom management.* New York: McGraw-Hill.

Wiles, J., & Bondi, J. (1998). *Curriculum development: A guide to practice* (5th ed.). Upper Saddle River, NJ: Merrill.

Winebrenner, S. (1992). *Teaching gifted kids in the regular classroom.* Minneapolis, MN: Free Spirit.

Wiseman, D. L., Cooner, D. D., & Knight, S. L. (1999). *Becoming a teacher in a field-based setting: An introduction to education and classrooms.* Belmont, CA: Wadsworth.

Wong, H. K., & Wong, R. T. (1998). *The first days of school: How to be an effective teacher* (2nd ed.). Mountain View, CA: Harry K. Wong.

Index

About the Author

Mary C. Clement was a high school Spanish and French teacher before earning a doctorate in curriculum and instruction at the University of Illinois at Urbana–Champaign in 1991. She served as the director of the Beginning Teacher Program at Eastern Illinois University for six years and is currently an assistant professor of education at Berry College, located 65 miles northwest of Atlanta, Georgia. Her current teaching schedule includes orientation to education classes, general secondary methods, foreign language methods, and graduate courses in curriculum. She has authored two books, *Building the Best Faculty* and *Put Your Oxygen Mask on First . . . and Other Strategies for Succeeding in Teaching*. Her articles have appeared in the *Kappan, Educational Forum, Educational Record, Contemporary Education,* and *The Clearinghouse.*

DATE DUE

DEC 2 2003		
MAR 3 1 2005		
April 22 2005		
OCT 3 1 2005		
APR 2 2 2009		
NOV 2 5 2008		
FEB 1 8 2009		
MAR 9 2009 OCT 1 8 2016		

Demco, Inc. 38-293